LONG ISLAND

GENEALOGICAL SOURCE MATERIAL

[A BIBLIOGRAPHY]

by

HERBERT F. SEVERSMITH, Ph.D., F.A.S.G.

and

KENN STRYKER-RODDA, Litt.D., F.A.S.G.

Published by

THE NATIONAL GENEALOGICAL SOCIETY

Arlington, Virginia

International Standard Book Number 0-915156-24-5

First Printing: 1962
Second Printing: 1980
Third Printing: 1987

Made in United States of America

FOREWORD

In February 1948, one of us (H.F.S.) gave a talk before the National Genealogical Society on Long Island genealogical source material, based upon personal bibliographic information collected to that date. The bibliography was published in the June 1948 issue of the *National Genealogical Society Quarterly*, Vol. XXXVI, No. 2, pp. 61-66, and subsequently reissued as *Genealogical Publication No. 9* of the National Genealogical Society. This is now out of print.

In the years since it has become evident that there is a very real demand for a more complete bibliographic index of Long Island genealogical source material (excluding family genealogies unless in compendiums). Accordingly, in 1958, the Council of the Society proposed to reprint *Publication No. 9* but, at the request of the original author, agreed to issue a revised and augmented edition. In the last two years and a half, the present authors have united their experience and efforts to this end, and the result is a bibliography increased from the original 125 references to 845 and more. Within the time allotted and the opportunities afforded, we have endeavored to make this compilation as complete as possible.

The reader should know, however, that whatever comprehensiveness the bibliography may possess, has been made possible because of the fine and sympathetic cooperation of our good friends. We wish particularly to mention the following: Mrs. Amy O. Bassford, Librarian of the Long Island Collection, the East Hampton, New York, Free Library; Mr. Archibald F. Bennett, Librarian and Secretary of the Utah Genealogical Society; Miss Edna Huntington, Librarian (retired), the Long Island Historical Society; Miss Pauline King, Assistant Librarian, the New England Historic Genealogical Society; Miss Marjorie Leek, Curator of the Long Island Collection, the Queens Borough, New York, Public Library; and Mrs. Mary Walsh, Librarian, the National Society of the Daughters of the American Revolution. We appreciate also the advice and suggestions received from our friends on the staff of the New York Genealogical and Biographical Society, the New York (City) Public Library and the Library of Congress. In the case of the last, we acknowledge the timely and expert assistance of the Union Catalog Division and of the librarians associated with Col. Willard Webb. Mr. Alvin R. L. Smith of Centereach, Long Island, is responsible for making available to us the analytic list of the Brookhaven Town Cemetery Book, and Miss Marjorie Leek has listed by location the cemetery inscriptions in the Frost and Meigs collections. We wish also to thank Mr. Wayne R. Stevenson of Bethesda, Maryland, for his patient and meticulous assistance in the preparation of the manuscript and the arrangement of the lists.

*   *   *   *   *

This book is divided into four parts: (1) a numbered, alphabetic bibliography by author wherever possible, otherwise by place, annotated with the Library of Congress Union Catalog symbols for libraries wherein the referenced book may be found; (2) an alphabetic listing of every referenced location, associated with the code numbers from the author list for that location; (3) an alphabetic listing of symbols employed by the Union Catalog Division of the Library of Congress, associated with the complete names of the libraries for which the symbols stand, and (4) an alphabetic list of the libraries to which reference is made. In the case of the symbols used for libraries, where entries have been taken from the *Union List of Serials,* the Library of Congress symbol has been substituted for those in the *List* when the latter are different.

And so, gentle reader, good luck and happy hunting!

H. F. S.
K. S.

Chevy Chase, Maryland, and
Brooklyn, New York

CONTENTS

A reader interested in locating material on a specific town, or a family that lived in a specific town, should turn first to Part II, where under the name of the town will be found the key index numbers of the books, articles, or manuscripts listed in Part I which contain information on that town. Then look in Part I for such number or numbers (shown in right margin), where the author and title will be found. Below each such entry are symbols indicating the libraries where the book or manuscript may be consulted. The names and locations of such libraries are shown in Part III.

BIBLIOGRAPHY OF SOURCES

Arranged by Author

Ackerly, Orville B(urnell). East Hampton, N. Y., Wills, 1665-1786. In *Ancient Long Island Epitaphs from the towns of Southold, Shelter Island and Easthampton* [!], *N. Y.* By Edward Doubleday Harris. [1

DLC, DNDAR, ICN, MBNEH, N, NBLiHi, NEh, NJQ, NN, NNNGB, NSmB, PHi, USlGS.

———— Early East Hampton Wills; abstracts from the New York (county) Surrogate's office. In *New York Geneal. and Biog. Record, 55*, pp. 200-208. [2

Az, C, CaOTP, CL, CoD, CSf, Ct, CtHi, CtY, DLC, DNDAR, IaHi, IC, ICN, ICU, In, MB, MBAt, MBNEH, MdBP, MeHi, MH, MHi, Mi, MiD-B, MNF, MnHi, MnM, MoK, MoS, MWA, N, NB, NBLiHi, NBu, NBuG, Nc, NEh, Nh, NHC, NHi, NIC, NjNbS, NjPla, NJQ NN, NNC, NNNGB, NR, OC, OCHP, OCl, OClWHi, OHi, PEa, PEr, PHi, PPi, PPL, USlGS, Wa, WaS, WM.

———— Huntington, New York Vital Records. In *New York Geneal. and Biog. Record, 50,* pp. 72, 127. [3

Az, C, CaOTP, CL, CoD, CSf, Ct, CtHi, CtY, DLC, DNDAR, IaHi, IC, ICN, ICU, In, MB, MBAt, MBNEH, MdBP, MeHi, MH, MHi, Mi, MiD-B, MNF, MnHi, MnM, MoK, MoS, MWA, N, NB, NBLiHi, NBu, NBuG, Nc, NEh, Nh, NHC, NHi, NIC, NjNbS, NjPla, NJQ, NN, NNC, NNNGB, NR, OC, OCHP, OCl, OClWHi, OHi, PEa, PEr, PHi, PPi, PPL, USlGS, Wa, WaS, WM.

———— Long Island cemeteries (various). Copies of tombstone inscriptions. (Scrapbook.) [4

NEh.

———— Copy of the tombstone inscriptions in old St. John's (Episcopal) Churchyard at Oakdale. Also list of burials from St. John's Church. (Typed.) [5

NBLiHi, NNNGB.

———— Contents of the "Small Book of Deeds" from the Southampton Town Clerk's office deposited in the Suffolk County Clerk's office, April 9, 1877. Transcribed in 1879. [6

NBLiHi, NEh, NNNGB (microfilm).

———— Ackerly deed books, Suffolk County. Vols. 1-17, 19 (photostats). [7

NEh.

———— Index of Suffolk County wills and administrations, 1787-1880. (Typed.) [8

NBLiHi.

Adams, James Truslow. Memorials of Old Bridgehampton. 1916.   [9
Includes records of the Old Cemetery, Main Street, Bridgehampton; Hayground Cemetery; Mecox Cemetery; Poxabogue Cemetery and Sagg Cemetery.
DLC, DNDAR, MBNEH, MH, N, NBLiHi, NEh, NHuHi, NJQ, NN, NNNGB, NRvS, NSmB.

———— History of the town of Southampton (east of Canoe Place). 1918.
[10
DLC, MB, MBNEH, MiU, MnU, MWA, N, NBB, NBLiHi, NHu, NJQ, NN, NNNGB, OClWHi.

Akerly, Lucy D(ubois). Inscriptions from the cemetery in Orient, L. I. Handwritten transcription made in 1922.   [11
NNNGB.

———— Southold, New York. Town records, vital statistics from libers D and E, in the Town Clerk's office. In *New York Geneal. and Biog. Record, 38,* pp. 164, 246; *39,* pp. 58, 129.   [12
Az, C, CaOTP, CL, CoD, CSf, Ct, CtHi, CtY, DLC, DNDAR, IaHi, IC, ICN, ICU, In, MB, MBAt, MBNEH, MdBP, MeHi, MH, MHi, Mi, MiD-B, MNF, MnHi, MnM, MoK, MoS, MWA, N, NB, NBLiHi, NBu, NBuG, Nc, NEh, Nh, NHC, NHi, NIC, NjNbS, NiPla, NJQ, NN. NNC, NNNGB, NR, OC, OCHP, OCl, OClWHi, OHi, PEa, PEr, PHi, PPi, PPL, USlGS, Wa, WaS, WM.

———— Vital Records of Suffolk County, N. Y. Transcribed.   [13
NNNGB.

Allen, Louise R. Inscriptions from an old Dutch cemetery on the estate of R. Clifford Monfort, Port Washington, New York. 1935. (Typed.)
NNNGB.   [14

Allen's Directory. Jamaica village and Richmond Hill directory. 1897.
MWA.   [15

Aquebogue, New York. A book of church records relating to the church of Aquebogue. (MS.)   [16
NNNGB.

Armbruster, Eugene L. The Eastern District of Brooklyn with illustrations and maps. 1912.   [17
DLC, MBNEH, MWA, N, NB, NBC, NBLiHi, NEh, NHu, NjNbS, NJQ, NN, NNNGB, NNUT, PP, PPL.

———— Brooklyn's Eastern District (East New York). 1942.   [18
DLC, NBC, NBLiHi, NEh, NJQ, NN.

———— Bushwick and her neighbors. (Scrapbooks.) 3 vols.   [19
NBLiHi.

———— Families of Jamaica, New York. (MS, package.)   [20
NBLiHi.

———— Historical data relating to places and families of Jamaica, New York. (MS, 3 packages.)   [21
NBLiHi.

———— Marriages of Long Island settlers and allied families. 3 vols. (Typed.) 1941. [22
NJQ.

———— Marriages on Long Island. (MS, 2 packages.) [23
NBLiHi.

———— Genealogical notes on families of Newtown and adjacent localities. (MS collection.) [24
NBLiHi.

———— Suffolk County. Scrapbooks made by Eugene L. Armbruster. 2 vols. [25
NBLiHi.

Astoria: First Reformed Church. An account of the first hundred years of the life and growth of the First Reformed Church, Astoria, Long Island, 1839-1939. [26
NBLiHi, NN, OCl.

Astoria, New York. Local papers of Astoria, 1833-1875. (One box.) [27
NHi.

Bailey, Paul. Long Island, a history of two great counties, Nassau and Suffolk. 3 vols., 1949. [28
DLC, NBLiHi, NEh, NJQ, NN, NNNGB; and "In all town libraries on Long Island": communication from Mr. Bailey.

Baldwin, Evelyn Briggs. List of colonial settlers and transcripts of town records, 1646-1705, of Gravesend, Kings County, N. Y. (MS.) 1917. NNNGB. [29

———— Cemetery Inscriptions in the Buffet Burying Ground, Dix Hills, New York. Transcript. [30
DLC, NNNGB, USlGS.

———— Smithtown, New York, First Presbyterian Church records, 1751-1867. In *New York Geneal. and Biog. Record, 42,* pp. 128, 272. [31
Az, C, CaOTP, CL, CoD, CSf, Ct, CtHi, CtY, DLC, DNDAR, IaHi, IC, ICN, ICU, In, MB, MBAt, MBNEH, MdBP, MeHi, MH, MHi, Mi, MiD-B, MNF, MnHi, MnM, MoK, MoS, MWA, N, NB, NBLiHi, NBu, NBuG, Nc, NEh, Nh, NHC, NHi, NIC, NjNbS, NjPla, NJQ, NN, NNC, NNNGB, NR, OC, OCHP, OCl, OClWHi, OHi, PEa, PEr, PHi, PPI, PPL, USlGS, Wa, WaS, WM.

Bangs, Charlotte Rebecca (Woglum). Reminiscences of old New Utrecht and Gowanus. 1912. [32
DLC, DNDAR, MBNEH, N, NBC, NBLiHi, NEh, NJQ, NN, NNG, NNNGB, OClWHi.

Barber, Gertrude A. Index of Wills probated in Kings County, New York, from January 1, 1850 to December 31, 1890. Transcript from original records. 1949. 3 vols. (Typed.) [33
ICN, NBLiHi, NBuG, NN, NNNGB.

———— North Beach, New York. The Riker and Luyster Cemeteries. In *Long Island Cemetery Inscriptions.* 1923. [34
DLC, MBNEH, NBLiHi, NNNGB, USlGS.

———————— Steinway, Long Island City, New York. The Lawrence Cemetery. In *Long Island Cemetery Inscriptions.* 1923.   [35
DLC, MBNEH, NBLiHi, NNNGB, USlGS.

———————— Births, marriages and deaths of Suffolk County, taken from the *Republican Watchman,* the *Long Island Traveler,* and the *South Side Signal,* 1867-1901. (Scrapbooks.) 3 vols.   [36
NBLiHi.

———————— Deaths in Suffolk County, New York, taken from the *Republican Watchman* of Greenport, Long Island, 1859-1900. 2 vols. 1949. (Typed.)   [37
NBuG, NN, NNNGB.

———————— Marriages of Suffolk County, New York, taken from the *Republican Watchman* of Greenport, Long Island, 1871-1901, and from two other newspapers. 1950. (Typed.)   [38
IHi, NBLiHi, NN.

———————— Woodside, New York: the Moore Cemetery. In *Long Island Cemetery Inscriptions.* 1923.   [39
DLC, MBNEH, NBLiHi, NNNGB, USlGS.

Barck, Dorothy C., editor. Papers of the Lloyd Family of the Manor of Queens Village, 1656-1826. In *Collections of the New York Historical Society, 59,* pp. 319-334.   [40
C, CaOTP, CaOTU, CSt, Ct, CtHT, CtW, CtY, CU, DLC, DNDAR, ICN, ICU, IEN, InU, IU, MA, MB, MBAt, MBNEH, MdBJ, MdBP, MH, MHi, MiD-B, MiU, MiU-C, MNF, MnHi, MNS, MnU, N, NB, NBLiHi, NBuG, NEh, NHC, NIC, NjP, NjPla, NJQ, NN, NNA, NNC, NNG, NNM, NNNGB, NNUT, NPV, OCl, OO, OU, PPAmP, PHi, PPi, PU, USlGS, WaU.

Bartlett, Elizabeth (French): (Elizabeth French). Huntington, New York Cemetery Inscriptions (St. John's Episcopal Churchyard). In *New Eng. Hist. Geneal. Register, 66,* p. 226.   [41
Az, C, CL, CoD, CSt, Ct, CtHi, CtHT, CtY, CU, DCU, DLC, DNDAR, GA, GHi, ICN, ICU, In, InI, IU, KHi, KyLoF, M, MB, MBAt, MBC, MBNEH, MdBE, MdBP, Me, MeB, MeBa, MeHi, MeP, MH, MHi, Mi, MiD-B, MiGr, MiMu, MiU, MiU-C, MNF, MnHi, MoK, MoS, MPB, MWA, MWiW, N, NBLiHi, NbO, NBu, Nc, NEh, NhD, NHi, NIC, NjP, NjPla, NJQ, NjR, NN, NNC, NNNGB, NNS, NNU-H, NR, OC, OCHP, OCl, OClWHi, OHi, OMC, OrP, PEa, PEr, PHi, PPi, PPL, PWb, RP, T, TC, Tx, USlGS, Vi, Wa, WaS, WHi, WM.

———————— Northport, New York Cemetery Inscriptions. In *New Eng. Hist. Geneal. Register, 66,* p. 226.   [42
Az, C, CL, CoD, CSt, Ct, CtHi, CtHT, CtY, CU, DCU, DLC, DNDAR, GA, GHi, ICN, ICU, In, InI, IU, KHi, KyLoF, M, MB, MBAt, MBC, MBNEH, MdBE, MdBP, Me, MeB, MeBa, MeHi, MeP, MH, MHi, Mi, MiD-B, MiGr, MiMu, MiU, MiU-C, MNF, MnHi, MoK, MoS, MPB, MWA, MWiW, N, NBLiHi, NbO, NBu, Nc, NEh, NhD, NHi, NIC, NjP, NjPla, NJQ, NjR, NN, NNC, NNNGB, NNS, NNU-H, NR, OC, OCHP, OCl, OClWHi, OHi, OMC, OrP, PEa, PEr, PHi, PPi, PPL, PWb, RP, T, TC, Tx, USlGS, Vi, Wa, WaS, WHi, WM.

Baxter, John. Journal of John Baxter of Flatlands, Long Island, 1790-1826, continued by his son, Garret Stoothoff Baxter, 1826-1835. Copied and indexed by Edna Huntington, Harriet Stryker-Rodda and Kenn Stryker-Rodda. 6 vols. (Typed.)   [43
NBLiHi.

Beck, Walter and Dudley Case. Queens County, New York: Wills of Real Estate, libers A—, 1787-1835, abstracted and indexed. (Typed.) [44 NJQ.

Beers, J. B. and Co. Atlas of Long Island, New York, from recent and actual surveys and records. 1873. [45 DLC, N, NBLiHi, NEh, NHu, NHuHi, NIC-A, NJQ, NN, NNC, NRvS, NSmB.

Bellot, Alfred Henry. History of the Rockaways from the year 1685 to 1917. 1918. [46 DLC, DNDAR, MWA, N, NB, NBLiHi, NEh, NJQ, NN, NNNGB.

Bensel, A. A. The Columbia Press Co.'s East Long Island directory. 1889/90. [47 NN.

Bergen, Teunis G(arret). Inscriptions from the burying ground of the Protestant Reformed Dutch Church of Bushwick and the Schenck family plot. [48 NBLiHi.

———— Lefferts and Vechte family burying grounds (Bushwick, New York). Inscriptions copied about 1863. (Typed.) [49 NBLiHi.

———— Records of Births in the Town Records at Gravesend. In *New York Geneal. and Biog. Record, 4,* p. 39. [50 Az, C, CaOTP, CL, CoD, CSf, Ct, CtHi, CtY, DLC, DNDAR, IaHi, IC, ICN, ICU, In, MB, MBAt, MBNEH, MdBP, MeHi, MH, MHi, Mi, MiD-B, MNF, MnHi, MnM, MoK, MoS, MWA, N, NB, NBLiHi, NBu, NBuG, Nc, NEh, Nh, NHC, NHi, NIC, NjNbS, NjPla, NJQ, NN, NNC, NNNGB, NR, OC, OCHP, OCl, OClWHi, OHi, PEa, PEr, PHi, PPi, PPL, USlGS, Wa, WaS, WM.

———— Gravesend burial ground inscriptions. Transcribed about 1868. NBLiHi. [51

———— Kings County, New York. Genealogical abstracts from town and church records, etc. (MS.) [52 NN (Manuscript Room).

———— Kings County, New York. Abstracts of miscellaneous Kings County wills, 1658-1869. 1 vol. [53 NJQ.

———— Register in Alphabetical Order, of the Early Settlers of Kings County, New York. 1881. [54 DLC, DNDAR, MBNEH, MdBP, MH, MWA, N, NBLiHi, NcD, NcU, NEh, Nh, NHu, NJQ, NN, NNG, NNNGB, OClWHi, PHi, PPL, USlGS.

———— Collections of military papers . . . of the 241st New York Regiment. Muster Rolls. [Brooklyn, New York.] [55 NJQ.

———— Genealogical memoranda mainly from church and family records (Long Island). 4 vols. (MS.) [56 NJQ.

————, editor. Genealogies of the state of New York . . . Long Island edition. 1915.   [57
NBLiHi, NN, NNNGB.

———— Inscriptions from the burying grounds of the Protestant Refor-med Dutch Church of New Lots. (MS and typed copy.) Also published in *Long Island Hist. Soc. Quarterly, 2,* pp. 52-54, 88-89, 112-113; *3,* pp. 20-21, 84-85; *4,* pp. 18-21.   [58
CoD, Ct, CtY, CU, DLC, DSI-M, ICN, IU, MeU, MH, MHi, MiD-B, MnHi, MWA, N, NB, NBB, NBLiHi, NBP, NBuG, NEh, NJQ, NjP, NN, NNC, OHi, PCA, PHi, VW, WaU, WHi.

———— History of New Utrecht, Long Island (1657-1857) (with gene-alogies of early families). (MS and 7 vols., copy.)   [59
NBLiHi.

———— New Utrecht Methodist Church burying ground. Inscriptions. (MS and typed copy.)   [60
NBLiHi.

———— Papers concerning New Utrecht, collected by Teunis G. Bergen. (MS.)   [61
NBLiHi.

———— Inscriptions from the burying ground of the Protestant Re-formed Dutch Church of New Utrecht, with additional entries from the sexton's book, with later inscriptions copied by Edna Huntington. (Typed.)   [62
NBLiHi.

Bethpage, New York. Cemetery records.   [63
NEh.

———— Powell Cemetery records.   [64
NEh.

Betts, Beverly R. Inscriptions from Tombstones in the Parish Church-yard at Jamaica, New York. In *New York Geneal. and Biog. Record, 7,* p. 18.   [65
Az, C, CaOTP, CL, CoD, CSf, Ct, CtHi, CtY, DLC, DNDAR, IaHi, IC, ICN, ICU, In, MB, MBAt, MBNEH, MdBP, MeHi, MH, MHi, Mi, MiD-B, MNF, MnHi, MnM, MoK, MoS, MWA, N, NB, NBLiHi, NBu, NBuG, Nc, NEh, Nh, NHC, NHi, NIC, NjNbS, NjPla, NJQ, NN, NNC, NNNGB, NR, OC, OCHP, OCl, OClWHi, OHi, PEa, PEr, PHi, PPi, PPL, USlGS, Wa, WaS, WM.

Blank, John. The census of 1781. *Nassau County Hist. Jour. 13:* 1, 39.
NBLiHi, NJQ, NN, NNNGB.   [66

Bogert, Henry L. Data on Manhattan and Brooklyn farms, with maps, etc. (MS.)   [67
NNNGB.

Bogert, J. H. Records of the Dutch Reformed Church of Wolver Hollow in Oyster Bay. (Baptisms, 1741-1834; marriages, 1826-1835; burials, 1777-1860.) (Typed.)   [68
NNNGB.

Bowne, Jacob T. Inscriptions from old cemeteries in Glen Cove. 1867. (MS.) [69
NNNGB.

Bowne, John. Diary of John Bowne, 1649-1677. (Flushing, New York.) NHi. [70

Bowne, John and **Samuel Bowne.** Account books of John and Samuel Bowne, Flushing, 1649-1703. (MS.) [71
NN (Manuscript Room).

Boyd, W. H. Boyd's Brooklyn business directory. [72
MWA, 1858/59, 1860; NBLiHi, 1858/59, 1860.

Boyd's Directory Co. Flushing directory; Flushing village directory; Flushing journal (title varies). Published in 1887/88 by F. A. Richmond and Co. [73
MWA, 1887/88, 1890/91; NB, 1885/86; NBLiHi, 1885/86; 1891/92; 1895/96; NJQ, 1879, 1893/4, 1897/98; NN, 1887/88, 1889/90.

———— Long Island business directory. (Imprint of publisher varies: Boyd's directory of . . . Long Island; Curtin's directory of . . . Long Island; Curtin's Brooklyn business directory, together with general directory of . . . Long Island; Lain's directory of Long Island; Boyd's Long Island business directory.) [74
DLC, 1864/65-1865/66, 1868/69, 1874/75; MWA, 1864/65, 1868/69, 1871/72; NB, 1865/66; NBLiHi, 1864/65, 1868/69, 1872/73-1873/74, 1878/79; NJQ, 1867/68-1868-69; NN, 1868/69-1872/73, 1874/75, 1876/77-1878/79, 1888/89; NRvS, 1865/66; NSmB, 1864/65-1865/66.

Bradlee, Thomas. Justice of the Peace, Jamaica, N. Y. Docket, 1861-1866. 2 vols. Some marriage records. (MS.) [75
NJQ.

Bridgehampton, New York. Bridgehampton. Justices of the Peace: Docket, Aug. 1848-May 1855. 2 vols. (MS.) [76
NJQ.

———— Bridgehampton Presbyterian Church records, 1823-1924. (Baptisms, marriages and deaths; and parish records to 1853.) (Typed.) "Mrs. Emma Morris copy". [77
NBLiHi.

Bronson family. Bronson family papers, 1760-1838. (Kings County.) (MS.) [78
NN (Manuscript Room).

Brookhaven, Town of. Records of the town of Brookhaven, Suffolk County, New York, from 1798 to March 1856, including Port Jefferson. Issued by the Town. [79
DLC, MB, MBNEH, MdBP, MWA, N, NBLiHi, NcD, NEh, Nh, NHu, NJQ, NN, NNC, NNNGB, NRvS, NSmB, PHi.

————— Records of the town of Brookhaven, Suffolk County, New York, from 1856 to December, 1885. Issued by the Town.   [80
DLC, MB, MBNEH, MdBP, MWA, N, NBLiHi, NcD, NEh, Nh, NHu, NJQ, NN, NNC, NNNGB, NRvS, NSmB, PHi.

————— Abstracts of wills, letters of administration of intestates of Brookhaven, L. I., on record in the office of the Suffolk County Clerk. (MS.)   [81
NNNGB.

Brooklyn, New York. Assessment books, 1841. (MS.)   [82
NBLiHi.

————— Atlas of the entire city of Brooklyn, from actual surveys and official records. G. W. Bromley and Company, 1880.   [83
DLC, NB, NBLiHi, NJQ, NN.

————— Inscriptions from the Cemetery at Boerum and Livingston Streets, 1803-1816. (Typed.)   [84
NBLiHi.

————— The Bushwick Avenue German Presbyterian Church. Confirmations, members admitted, and contributions, 1881-1887. (MS.)
NJQ.   [85

————— The Cedar Street Methodist Episcopal Church. Members, baptisms, marriages, etc. 1873-1893. 3 vols. (MS.)   [86
NBLiHi.

————— Central Congregational Church. Roll of Members, 1896. (MS.)
NBLiHi.   [87

————— The Brooklyn city directory, 1822-1933/4. The imprint varies: Brooklyn directory; Brooklyn directory and yearly advertiser; Spooner's Brooklyn directory; Brooklyn alphabetical and street directory and yearly advertiser; Hearnes' Brooklyn city directory; Smith's Brooklyn directory; The Brooklyn city directory; The Brooklyn city and business directory; Lain's Brooklyn directory; Lain and Healy's Brooklyn directory; Brooklyn general directory; Upington's general directory of Brooklyn; Upington's general directory of the borough of Brooklyn; Polk's Brooklyn (New York) city directory. No directories were issued in 1827-28, 1911, 1914-32.   [88
DLC, 1823, 1825, 1838/39, 1841/42-1846/47, 1848/49-1857/58, 1860/61, 1862/63-1933/34; MWA, 1839/40-1841/42, 1843/44-1867/68, 1868/69-1879/80, 1881/82-1913; N, 1822, 1825, 1831/32, 1834/35, 1836/37, 1838/39-1871/72, 1873/74-1884/85, 1886/87-1887/88, 1890/91-1893/94, 1895/96-1933/34; NBB, 1855/56-1856/57; NBLiHi, 1822-1830, 1832/33-1858/59, 1860/61-1863/64, 1865/66-1933/34; NIC, 1876/77, 1892/93; NJQ, 1842/43-1844/45, 1846/47, 1848/49, 1850/51-1851/52, 1853/54, 1855/56-1856/57, 1862/63, 1864/65-1865/66, 1868/69-1869/70, 1873/74-1874/75, 1880/81, 1882/83, 1884/85-1887/88, 1889/90-1891/92, 1893/94-1897/98, 1899/1900, 1901/02-1907, 1909-1933/34; NN, 1822-1913, 1933 (microfilm, 30 reels; also includes Brooklyn pages from New York directories of 1796, 1802/3 and 1811/12) ; NNC, 1854/55, 1863/64, 1933/34; NNNGB, 1843-1877 (22 vols.); NSmB, 1823, 1845/46-1846/47, 1848/49-1849/50.

————— Cook Street (Bushwick) Methodist Episcopalian Church records. Probationers, 1842-1856, 1866-1891; members, 1880-1891; baptisms, 1841-1861, 1866-1891; marriages, 1846-1857, 1866-1891. (MS.)   [89
NBLiHi.

———— Brooklyn deaths, 1847-1853; 1857-1861, and births, 1869. [90
NNNGB.

———— Brooklyn deaths, 1847-1850, 1853-1865, in libers, with cemetery
of interment. Also card index of deaths, 1847-1871. [91
KINGS COUNTY CLERK'S OFFICE, BROOKLYN.

———— Abstracts of deeds to old Brooklyn farms. (MS.) [92
NBLiHi.

———— English Evangelical Lutheran Church of the Reformation. The
first forty years, 1898-1938; includes baptisms, marriages and deaths.
NJQ, NN. [93

———— First Methodist Episcopal Church of Brooklyn. Baptisms,
1796-1883; marriages, 1802-1886; deaths, 1807-1808; members, 1798-
1816. [94
NNNGB (microfilm).

———— First Methodist Episcopal Church. Class register, 1850. (MS.)
NBLiHi. [95

———— First Reformed Dutch Church of Brooklyn, New York. Records
(earliest known). *The Holland Society Year Book*, 1897. [96
DLC, DNDAR, MBNEH, NBLiHi, NEh, NJQ, NN, NNHol, NNNGB, USlGS.

———— First Reformed Dutch Church of Brooklyn, New York. Register
of Baptisms, 1792-1794. (Typed.) [97
NBLiHi.

———— First Reformed Dutch Church of Brooklyn, New York. Handwritten data in Dutch relating to pew holders, about 1770. [98
NNNGB.

———— History of the First Reformed Protestant Dutch Church of
Breuckelen, now known as the First Reformed Church of Brooklyn,
1654 to 1696. Compiled by order of the Consistory. 1896. [99
DLC, NB, NBLiHi, NJQ, NN, NNUT.

———— Fort Greene Cemetery inscriptions, 1821. [100
NBLiHi.

———— The Greene Avenue Baptist Church, Brooklyn. Records, 1854 to
1945. 7 vols. (MS.) [101
NBLiHi.

———— Records of the Holy Trinity (Episcopal) Church of Brooklyn.
Baptisms, marriages and deaths from 1841. [102
NNNGB (microfilm).

———— Household of Faith Church, Brooklyn. Records, 1879-1922. 6
vols. (MS.) [103
NBLiHi.

———— Lee Avenue Sabbath School, Brooklyn. Marriages and deaths,
1858-1860. (Typed.) [104
NBLiHi.

———— List of Persons of Brooklyn who reported income, 1865. Mounted clippings from the Brooklyn *Daily Union*.   [105
NBLiHi.

———— Local papers of Brooklyn, 1681-1854. 1 box. (MS.)   [106
NHi.

———— Duplicates of original marriage certificates from the Bureau of Vital Statistics in Brooklyn. May, 1866-Nov., 1872 and 1879.   [107
NNNGB.

———— Index to marriages performed by mayors of Brooklyn, 1839-1887. (Typed.)   [108
NBLiHi.

———— The Church of Our Lady of Victory: Records of subscribers, 1868. (MS.)   [109
NBLiHi.

———— Inscriptions from the cemetery at the Naval Hospital (Brooklyn, New York). (Partial record.) (Typed.)   [110
NBLiHi.

———— Pacific Street Methodist Episcopal Church records. Baptisms and probationers, 1857-1890; marriages, 1846-1890; members, 1849-1890, and various minute books. (MS.)   [111
NBLiHi.

———— Records of the Church of the Pilgrims, from 1844. Baptisms, marriages, deaths and lists of members.   [112
NNNGB (microfilm).

———— St. Paul's Free Church. Accounts, 1834-1840. (MS.)   [113
NBLiHi.

———— Records of the Second Presbyterian Church, 1831-1922 (?).
NN (microfilm).   [114

———— Throop Avenue Presbyterian Church records. Confirmations, 1874-1887, by-laws and minutes of the Women's Society, 1870-1877 (in German). (MS.)   [115
NJQ.

———— Throop Street Methodist Episcopal Church records. Probationers and members, 1887-1894; marriages, 1877-1891; baptisms 1887-1893, and various minute books. (MS.)   [116
NBLiHi.

———— Trinity Baptist Church, Brooklyn. Records, 1874-1915. (MS.)
NBLiHi.   [117

———— Washington Avenue Baptist Church, Brooklyn. Records, 1851-1925 (members, deaths, minutes, etc.). 2 vols. (MS.)   [118
NBLiHi.

———— Williamsburgh Station, Brooklyn Methodist Protestant Church. Minutes of quarterly conferences, 1834-1854 (some marriages and baptismal records, 1835-1838). (MS.)   [119
NJQ.

———— Willoughby Avenue Baptist Church, Brooklyn.   Records, 1879-
1884.   (MS.)   [120
NBLiHi.

———— York Street Methodist Episcopal Church records.   Members,
1850.   (MS.)   [121
NN   (Manuscript Room).

Brush, Frank E.   The records of Smithtown, Suffolk County (New York),
1917.   An inventory reprinted from the annual report of the state his-
torian.   [122
DLC, MWA, N, NBLiHi, NJQ, NN, NNNGB.

Bunker, Mary Powell (Seaman).   Long Island Genealogies, 1895.   [123
CSmH, CU, DLC, DNDAR, I, MBNEH, MdBP, MiU-C, MWA, N, NBLiHi, NEh,
NIC, NJQ, NN, NNNGB, OCl, OClWHi, PHC, PSC-Hi, USlGS.

———— Long Island Genealogies, 1895.   Additions in 1901 by the author.
Indexed by Edna Huntington.   [124
NBLiHi, NJQ.

Bushwick, New York.   Ancient Bushwick, with old Bushwick cemetery
inscriptions.   In *Long Island Weekly Star*, 31 December 1880.   Also a
typed copy.   [125
NBLiHi.

———— Ancient burial ground (inscriptions).   1861.   Transcript.   [126
NBLiHi.

———— Bushwick Reformed Church records.   Baptisms, marriages
1792-1876; members, 1789-1917.   (Typed.)   [127
NJQ   (microfilm), NNNGB   (microfilm).

———— Bushwick Reformed Church records.   Register of baptisms, marriages and deaths, 1821-1917.   3 vols.   (Typed.)   [128
NJQ.

———— Records of the Schenck family burying ground.   From a news-
paper clipping of 1880.   (Two of these gravestones are preserved in the
Museum of the City of New York.)   [129
NBLiHi.

Calkin-Kelly Directory Co.   Huntington, New York, directory, including
Huntington Station, Northport, East Northport.   1929.   [130
NJQ.

Callendar, James H.   Yesterdays on Brooklyn Heights, 1927.   [131
DLC, ICU, MB, MH, NB, NBB, NBLiHi, NJQ, NN, NNNGB, OClWHi, PU, ViU.

Canfield, Amos.   Town records of Newtown, Long Island (1659-1730).
In *New York Geneal. and Biog. Record, 63*, p. 359; *64*, p. 28.   (Gene-
alogical abstracts.)   [132
Az, C, CaOTP, CL, CoD, CSf, Ct, CtHi, CtY, DLC, DNDAR, IaHi, IC, ICN, ICU,
In, MB, MBAt, MBNEH, MdBP, MeHi, MH, MHi, Mi, MiD-B, MNF, MnHi, MnM,
MoK, MoS, MWA, N, NB, NBLiHi, NBu, NBuG, Nc, NEh, Nh, NHC, NHi, NIC,
NjNbS, NjPla, NJQ, NN, NNC, NNNGB, NR, OC, OCHP, OCl, OClWHi, OHi, PEa,
PEr, PHi, PPi, PPL, USlGS, Wa, WaS, WM.

———— Abstracts of Early Wills of Queens County, New York. Recorded in libers A and C of Deeds, the Register's Office at Jamaica, New York. In *New York Geneal. and Biog. Record, 65,* pp. 114, 245, 319.
[133

Az, C, CaOTP, CL, CoD, CSf, Ct, CtHi, CtY, DLC, DNDAR, IaHi, IC, ICN, ICU, In, MB, MBAt, MBNEH, MdBP, MeHi, MH, MHi, Mi, MiD-B, MNF, MnHi, MnM, MoK, MoS, MWA, N, NB, NBLiHi, NBu, NBuG, Nc, NEh, Nh, NHC, NHi, NIC, NjNbS, NjPla, NJQ, NN, NNC, NNNGB, NR, OC, OCHP, OCl, OClWHi, OHi, PEa, PEr, PHi, PPi, PPL, USlGS, Wa, WaS, WM.

Carpenter, Daniel H. Oyster Bay Baptist Church Marriages, 1802-1815. In *New York Geneal. and Biog. Record, 29,* p. 174.   [134

Az, C, CaOTP, CL, CoD, CSf, Ct, CtHi, CtY, DLC, DNDAR, IaHi, IC, ICN, ICU, In, MB, MBAt, MBNEH, MdBP, MeHi, MH, MHi, Mi, MiD-B, MNF, MnHi, MnM, MoK, MoS, MWA, N, NB, NBLiHi, NBu, NBuG, Nc, NEh, Nh, NHC, NHi, NIC, NjNbS, NjPla, NJQ, NN, NNC, NNNGB, NR, OC, OCHP, OCl, OClWHi, OHi, PEa, PEr, PHi, PPi, PPL, USlGS, Wa, WaS, WM.

———— Searingtown: Williams farm cemetery. In *New York Geneal. and Biog. Record, 25,* p. 146.   [135

Az, C, CaOTP, CL, CoD, CSf, Ct, CtHi, CtY, DLC, DNDAR, IaHi, IC, ICN, ICU, In, MB, MBAt, MBNEH, MdBP, MeHi, MH, MHi, Mi, MiD-B, MNF, MnHi, MnM, MoK, MoS, MWA, N, NB, NBLiHi, NBu, NBuG, Nc, NEh, Nh, NHC, NHi, NIC, NjNbS, NjPla, NJQ, NN, NNC, NNNGB, NR, OC, OCHP, OCl, OClWHi, OHi, PEa, PEr, PHi, PPi, PPL, USlGS, Wa, WaS, WM.

Carter, Edith M. Bible and cemetery records of Center Moriches, Long Island, 1957.   [136
NEh.

Case, Dudley. Queens County. Abstracts of personal wills, libers, 1-3, 1835-1875.   [137
NJQ (typescript) ; NNNGB (microfilm).

———— Queens County. Wills of real estate, 1834-1852, and personal wills, 1864-1875. (Abstracted.)   [138
NJQ (typescript) ; NNNGB (microfilm).

Case, J(oseph) Wickham, editor. Southold Town Records, 1651-1797. 1882, 1884. 2 vols.   [139
DLC, DNDAR, MBNEH, MWA, NBLiHi, NEh, NJQ, NN, NNNGB.

Cedar Swamp, New York. Miscellaneous items relating to Cedar Swamp, near Glen Cove. (MS.)   [140
NNNGB.

Chadbourne, Harriet Walters. My grandmother's stories *(re* Huntington during and after the Revolution) ; with genealogical notes on Long Island families.   [141
NN.

Chalmers, Rev. William I. Register of funerals, burials, marriages and baptisms conducted by the Rev. William I. Chalmers, 1872-1916. Riverhead, New York. (MS, with indexes.)   4 vols.   [142
NBLiHi.

———— Census of the New Church (Swedenborgian) cemetery at Riverhead. (MS.)   [143
NBLiHi.

Chapman Publishing Co. Portrait and biographical record of Queens
County, New York. Containing portraits and biographical sketches of
. . . citizens of the county. 1896.   [144
DLC, DNDAR, MBNEH, MWA, N, NBLiHi, NEh, NJQ, NN, NNNGB.

———— Portrait and biographical record of Suffolk County, New York.
Containing portraits and biographical sketches of . . . citizens of the
county. 1896.   [145
DLC, MWA, N, NBLiHi, NHu, NIC, NJQ, NN, NSmB.

Chase, Benjamin. Diary of Benjamin Chase, 1799-1811. Includes records of marriages and deaths at Cutchogue, New York, and in the
vicinity. (Typed.)   [146
NBLiHi.

Cleveland, Nathaniel Hubbard. The Salmon records: Cleveland supplement, 1812-1880. Photostats of newspaper clippings from the *Long Island Traveler*, 1879-82, and the *Suffolk Times*.   [147
NBLiHi, NN.

Cockcroft, Georgia C. (Mrs. James D.). Inscriptions from the old burying
ground at Crab Meadow, Huntington, New York. In *Long Island Hist.
Soc. Quarterly, 1*, pp. 116-117.   [148
CoD, Ct, CtY, CU, DLC, DSI-M, ICN, IU, MeU, MH, MHi, MiD-B, MnHi, MWA,
N, NB, NBB, NBLiHi, NBP, NBuG, NEh, NjP, NJQ, NN, NNC, OHi, PCA, PHi,
VW, WaU, WHi.

———— Inscriptions from the old Tilden plot in fields adjoining Selah
Brush's farm in Huntington (Greenlawn), Long Island. In *Long Is-
land Hist. Soc. Quarterly, 1*, p. 118.   [149
CoD, Ct, CtY, CU, DLC, DSI-M, ICN, IU, MeU, MH, MHi, MiD-B, MnHi, MWA,
N, NB, NBB, NBLiHi, NBP, NBuG, NEh, NjP, NJQ, NN, NNC, OHi, PCA, PHi,
VW, WaU, WHi.

———— Inscriptions from cemeteries in Nassau County. 1939. (Typed.)
COLD SPRING HARBOR: Cemetery above St. John's Episcopal Church.   [150
OYSTER BAY: Cemetery on Woodbury Road; Velsor plot, Woodbury Highway; ceme-
tery between Oyster Bay roads to East Norwich and Glen Cove; Christ's Church
cemetery; Schenck plot (Nostrand Avenue).
ROSLYN: Cemetery on North Hempstead turnpike.
SYOSSET: Cheshire plot.
NBLiHi.

———— The Smith Burying Ground on top of the hill, back of Miss Julia
A. Smith's home, Setauket, New York. In *Long Island Hist. Soc.
Quarterly, 1*, p. 81.   [151
CoD, Ct, CtY, CU, DLC, DSI-M, ICN, IU, MeU, MH, MHi, MiD-B, MnHi, MWA, N,
NB, NBB, NBLiHi, NBP, NBuG, NEh, NjP, NJQ, NN, NNC, OHi, PCA, PHi, VW,
WaU, WHi.

———— Inscriptions from cemeteries in Suffolk County. 1939. (Typed.)
CENTERPORT: Cemetery on Belcher farm.   [152
COMMACK: Burr Avenue, Brown, Harned-Seaman-Smith plots; Wicks cemetery;
cemetery on Highway Spur.

CRABMEADOW.

DIX HILLS: Carll farm cemetery; Dix Hills cemetery.

EAST HAMPTON: Edwards, Hubbard, and Ranger plots; plot off Three-Neck Harbor Road.

EAST NORTHPORT: Ketcham plot.

EATON'S NECK: Gardiner plot.

FIREPLACE: Parsons plot.

FORT SALONGA.

GARDINER'S ISLAND.

GREENLAWN: Tilden plot.

HUNTINGTON: Buffett, Burr, Gardiner, Nostrand and Rome plots; cemetery on Woodbury Road; Carman, Velsor and Woolsey plots; cemetery on the Colyer farm; private cemetery near Jericho turnpike.

KING'S PARK: Hallock, Miles and Vail family plots.

MANORVILLE: Raynor cemetery.

MECOX cemetery.

MELVILLE: Ketcham plot; Melville cemetery.

MIDDLEVILLE: Ketcham plot.

NISSEQUOGUE: Smith family cemetery.

NORTHPORT: Scidmore plot.

PATCHOGUE: Smith-Tuttle cemetery.

SMITH'S POINT.

SMITHTOWN: Smith and Thompson plots; cemetery on Islip Line Road; Smithtown Landing cemetery.

SOUTH GREENLAWN: Oakes plot.

SOUTH HUNTINGTON: Carll family cemetery; cemetery on Greenlawn Road; Smith Farm cemetery.

SWEZEYTOWN.

WYANDANCH: Conklin plot.

NBLiHi.

Cocks, George W. List of genealogies and families of Long Island origin. compiled by the late George W. Cocks of Glen Cove. (Cards.) [153
NN.

———— Record of marriages (1802-1855) and burials in the Baptist Church in Oyster Bay. 1905. [154
NNNGB.

———— Miscellany of old records of Oyster Bay (including Hog Island, Matinecock and Musketo Cove). 1895. (MS.) [155
NNNGB.

———— Oyster Bay Town Records, 1653-1878, compiled by George W. Cocks and compared and indexed by John Cox, Jr. 1916-40. 8 vols. [156
DLC, DNDAR, MBNEH, MWA, N, NBLiHi, NEh, NGlc, NHu, NJQ, NN, NNC, NNNGB, USlGS.

Cocks, George W., and Lucy D. Akerly. Tombstone inscriptions from Huntington and Smithtown. (Typed.) [157
NNNGB.

Cocks, George W., and W. A. Macy. Tombstone inscriptions of Smithtown and Huntington. (Typed.) [158
Cemetery on road to Ft. Salonga; cemetery near Sammis farm; cemetery at St. James or Mills Pond; Vail family plot at Kings Park; two family cemeteries near Kings Park hospital.
NBLiHi.

Cohen, Minnie (alias Cowen, Minnie). Greenwood cemetery inscriptions, Brooklyn, New York. 1932. 3 vols. (Typed.) [159
MBNEH, NBLiHi, NNNGB.

Cold Spring Harbor, New York. Inscriptions from a cemetery near St. John's Episcopal Church, Cold Spring Harbor. (MS.) [160
NNNGB.

The Cold Spring Harbor Village Improvement Society. Cold Spring Harbor Soundings. 1953. [161
DLC, NBLiHi, NEh, NJQ, NN.

Colonial Dames of the State of New York. Genealogical records . . . taken from family Bibles, 1581-1917. (Long Island.) 1917. [162
NJQ.

Combes, George D. Court notes and miscellaneous vital records of Hempstead . . . 1923. (MS.) [163
NNNGB.

———— Early Vital Records of Hempstead, Long Island, New York. In *New York Geneal. and Biog. Record, 54,* p. 42; *55,* pp. 270, 368; *56,* p. 19. [164
Az, C, CaOTP, CL, CoD, CSf, Ct, CtHi, CtY, DLC, DNDAR, IaHi, IC, ICN, ICU, In, MB, MBAt, MBNEH, MdBP, MeHi, MH, MHi, Mi, MiD-B, MNF, MnHi, MnM, MoK, MoS, MWA, N, NB, NBLiHi, NBu, NBuG, Nc, NEh, Nh, NHC, NHi, NIC, NjNbS, NjPla, NJQ, NN, NNC, NNNGB, NR, OC, OCHP, OCl, OClWHi, OHi, PEa, PEr, PHi, PPi, PPL, USIGS, Wa, WaS, WM.

Conklin, Sarah J. South End, cemetery inscriptions, East Hampton, 1933. (Typed.) [165
NBLiHi, NEh, NN.

The Connecticut Society of the Order of the Founders and Patriots of America. Vital Records of New Haven (Connecticut), 1649-1850. 1917. 2 vols. [166
Contains references to early settlers, particularly of Southold, Southampton, East Hampton and Brookhaven towns, New York.
DLC, MWA, NBLiHi, NN, NNNGB.

Couwenhoven family. Couwenhoven family papers, 1639-1773, and 1687-1850. (MS.) [167
References to various properties in Actevelt, Amesvoort, Gouanes and New Utrecht; settlements of various estates (*e.g.,* Cornelis Lambertse Cool).
NN (Manuscript Room).

Craven, Charles E(dmiston). A History of Mattituck, New York, 1906. [168
Includes the church baptismal records at Mattituck and Aquebogue, 1751-1776; marriages, 1751-1809; deaths, 1768-1809; and inscriptions in the parish burying ground at Mattituck, 1725-1905.
DLC, MB, MBNEH, MWA, N, NBLiHi, NEh, NHu, NjP, NJQ, NN, NNNGB, NRvS, NSmB, PHi, PPPrHi, USIGS.

Culver, Isabelle Terry. Genealogical data concerning the Conklin, Culver,

Homan and Terry families. (Long Island.)   [169
NEh.

Dankaerts, Jasper. Journal of a voyage to New York in 1679-80. [170
NBLiHi, (Dutch MS.); NBLiHi, NNNGB (translated and edited by Henry Mur-
phy, 1867); NNNGB (revised translation, edited by Bartlett Burleigh James and
J. Franklin Jameson, 1913).

Dayton, Alice. Tombstone inscriptions from cemeteries in the town of
East Hampton. North End cemetery, East Hampton, 1934. (Typed.)
NBLiHi, NEh.   [171

Daughters of the American Revolution, Rufus King Chapter. Family
Bible records, Jamaica, New York. 1938. (Typed.)   [172
NJQ.

Daughters of the American Revolution, Southampton Colony Chapter.
Bible records (Southampton, New York). 1939.   [173
NEh.

———— Bible records of the Conklin, Bishop, Glover, Parsons and Pier-
son families (Southampton, New York). 19—.   [174
NEh.

———— Tombstone inscriptions in Southampton and East Hampton
towns (outside East Hampton village). 1939.   [175
NEh.

———— Southampton births and baptisms. 1939.   [176
NEh.

———— Southampton marriage records. 1939.   [177
NEh.

———— Southampton mortuary records. 1939.   [178
NEh.

DeBevoise, Richard G(osman). Newtown, New York, First Reformed
Dutch Church. Baptisms and marriages. Vol. 1, 1736-1845; vol. 3,
1861-1935. Vol. 2 not reported. (Typed.)   [179
NJQ, NN.

———— Newtown, New York, First Reformed Dutch Church. Abstracts
from Minutes, 1848-1910; 1828-1861. (Typed.)   [180
NJQ.

Dering, Henry Packer. Henry Packer Dering papers, 1780-1855. [Sag
Harbor, New York.] (MS.)   [181
NN (Manuscript Room).

Dilliard, Maud Esther. Old Dutch Houses of Brooklyn. 1945.   [182
DLC, MB, MBNEH, NBC, NBLiHi, NEh, NJQ, NN, NNNGB, OOxM, ViU.

Ditmars, Chauncey L. C., and Maud E. Dilliard. Inscriptions from an old

cemetery at Montauk. 1928. (Typed.)   [183
NBLiHi.

Ditmas, Charles Andrew. Historic Homesteads of Kings County. [184
DLC, DNDAR, MB, MBNEH, MdBP, N, NBC, NBLiHi, NEh, NjNbS, NJQ, NN,
NNNGB.

Dripps, William C. Atlas of the townships of New Utrecht, Gravesend,
Flatbush, Flatlands and New Lots, Kings County, New York. 1877;
2nd ed., 1878.   [185
NBLiHi, NJQ.

Dubois, Rev. Anson. A History of the town of Flatlands, Kings County
New York. 1884.   [186
DLC, DNDAR, NBLiHi, NEh, NJQ.

Duryea, Charles and Alice Quinn Smith. Cemetery inscriptions, Brentwood. L. I. 1937. (Typed.)   [187
NBLiHi.

——— Cemetery inscriptions, Commack, L. I. 1937. (Typed.) [188
NBLiHi.

——— Private cemetery (inscriptions) at East Farmingdale. 1938.
(Typed.)   [189
NBLiHi.

Duvall, Ralph G. History of Shelter Island, 1652-1932.   [190
DLC, MB, MBNEH, MWA, N, NBLiHi, NcU, NEh, NHu, NJQ, NN, NNNGB, NRvS,
NSmB, PHC.

Dyson, Verne. A century of Brentwood, 1950. Also Supplement and index, with family history.   [191
NBLiHi, NJQ, NN, NNNGB.

——— History of Central Islip. 1954.   [192
Includes references to the earliest pioneers and to personalities of the present.
NBLiHi, NJQ, NN.

——— Deer Park—Wyandanch History. 1957.   [193
NBLiHi, NJQ, NN.

Eardeley, James Wadsworth. (Inscriptions in) St. James Roman Catholic
Church cemetery at Jay and Chapel Streets, Brooklyn. 1914. (Typed.)
NBLiHi.   [194

——— (Inscriptions in) The New Lots Reformed Dutch Cemetery, and
St. Marks Protestant Episcopal Church cemetery, New York City.
1914. (MS.)   [195
NBLiHi.

——— Federal census of Queens County, 1850. (Typed.)   [196
NBLiHi, NJQ, NN, NNNGB (microfilm).

——— Inscriptions from St. Matthews Protestant Episcopal cemetery,
Woodhaven, 1793-1892. 1914. (Typed.)   [197
NBLiHi.

———— Tombstone inscriptions from an old abandoned cemetery on old Bowery Bay Road, near Northern Blvd., Woodside. 1923. (Typed.)
NBLiHi.   [198

Eardeley, William A(pplebie) (Daniel). Seven Cemeteries, village of Amityville, town of Babylon, New York; and Bible records, 1813-1913. 1913. (Typed.)   [199
Oakwood Corp. cem. 1813-1912; Old Town, Ketchem, Payne, Purdy, Chichester and Bayview Avenue cemeteries; Bible records.
DLC, NBLiHi, NJQ, NN, USIGS.

———— Lawrence family cemetery at Astoria. 1924. (MS.)   [200
NBLiHi.

———— Three cemeteries, Bethpage and Farmingdale, town of Oyster Bay, Queens County, now Nassau County, Long Island, N. Y., 1832-1898. 1918. (Typed.)   [201
NBLiHi, NJQ, NN.

———— Brookhaven, New York, Cemetery Inscriptions: Brookfield (Manorville) cemetery. (Typed.)   [202
NBLiHi.

———— Brookhaven, New York, Cemetery Inscriptions. Dering Place cemetery. (Typed.)   [203
NBLiHi.

———— Brookhaven, New York, Cemetery Inscriptions. East Setauket Cemetery. (Typed.)   [204
NBLiHi.

———— Brookhaven, New York, Cemetery Inscriptions. Lake Grove Methodist cemetery. (Typed.)   [205
NBLiHi.

———— Brookhaven, New York, Cemetery Inscriptions. Millers Place cemetery; Miller burying ground, Witches Rock. (Typed.)   [206
NBLiHi.

———— Brookhaven, New York, Cemetery Inscriptions. St. James Mills burial ground at Mills Pond. (Typed.)   [207
NBLiHi.

———— Brookhaven, New York, Cemetery Inscriptions. Mount Sinai cemeteries. (Typed.)   [208
Bayles, Smith Davis, Victor Floyd Davis, Timothy Davis and Samuel Davis family cemeteries.
NBLiHi.

———— Brookhaven, New York, Cemetery Inscriptions. Roe plot, Cedar Hill cemetery, Port Jefferson. (Typed.)   [209
NBLiHi.

———— Brookhaven, New York, Cemetery Inscriptions. Hallock burying ground at Rocky Point. (Typed.)   [210
NBLiHi.

———— Brookhaven, New York, Cemetery Inscriptions. Hawkins and Roe plots, Selden. (Typed.)   [211
NBLiHi.

———— Brookhaven, New York, Cemetery Inscriptions. George Elder Vines, Thompson, and Biggs burial grounds, Setauket. (Typed.) [212 NBLiHi.

———— Brookhaven, New York, Cemetery Inscriptions. Hawkins, Davis, and Methodist cemeteries, Stony Brook. (Typed.) [213 NBLiHi.

———— Canarsie cemetery inscriptions. 1916. (Typed.) [214 NBLiHi.

———— Flatbush Reformed Dutch Church cemetery, 1754-1913. 1913. (Typed.) [215 NB, NBLiHi, NN.

———— Flushing, Queens County, Long Island, New York, monthly meeting of Friends. Intentions of marriage, 1704-1776. 1913. (Typed.) DLC, NBLiHi, NJQ, NN (and microfilm). [216

———— Village of Freeport, town of Hempstead, County of Nassau, Long Island, New York. Presbyterian Church cemetery, 1818 to 1911. 1913. (Typed.) [217 DLC, NBLiHi, NJQ, NN, NNNGB, USlGS.

———— Cornell family cemeteries (inscriptions), Hempstead. (Typed.) NBLiHi. [218

———— Trinity Episcopal Church, Hewlett, Long Island: Excerpts from burial, baptismal and marriage records. (MS.) [219 NBLiHi.

———— Rural cemetery inscriptions, Huntington. 1914. (Typed.) [220
Includes also stones removed there from the Lloyd graveyard at Lloyd's Neck (1719-1904), the Place graveyard at Melville (1868-1907) and the Brush graveyard at West Hills (1764-1901). Also genealogical items on the Brush, Higbie, Lloyd and Rogers families.
DLC, NBLiHi, NJQ, NN, USlGS.

———— Records in the office of the County Clerk at Jamaica, Long Island, 1680-1781. Wills and administrations, guardians and inventories. 1918. 2 vols. (Typed.) [221 NJQ, NN.

———— Cemeteries in Kings and Queens Counties, Long Island, New York, 1753-1913. 1916. (Typed.) [222
BROOKLYN: Humboldt Street cemetery, 1801-1831.
CANARSIE cemetery, 1832-1902.
ELMONT: Old cemetery, formerly Foster's Meadow, 1753-1909, and St. John's Methodist cemetery, 1819-1913.
JAMAICA: First Methodist cemetery, 1816-1912.
NEW UTRECHT: Bay Ridge cemetery, 1788-1841.
WOODHAVEN: St. Matthews Protestant Episcopal cemetery, 1793-1892; notes on Woodhaven families.
DLC, DNDAR, NBLiHi, NJQ, NN, USlGS.

———— Genealogical notes of 23 Long Island families. Twenty-three envelopes of manuscript notes on the following families: Bedell, Carman, Conklin, Cornell, Davis, DeMott, Hendrickson, Hewlett, Hicks, Hulse, Lamberson, Langdon, Miller, Osman, Pettit, Remsen, Rhodes,

Roe, Southard, Thorne, Tuthill, Weeks, and Wiltsie. (MS.)   [223
NJQ.

———— Inscriptions from the Sand Hole Cemetery (Methodist Church),
Lynbrook, Long Island. 1923. (Typed.)   [224
NBLiHi.

———— Inscriptions from the Presbyterian Churchyard, Middle Island,
Brookhaven. 1922. (Typed).   [225
NBLiHi.

———— New Utrecht Reformed Dutch Church cemetery. Inscriptions.
(Typed.)   [226
NBLiHi.

———— Abstracts of wills recorded in Surrogates' offices at county seats
in New York state. (MS, with analytic card index.) To 1840.   [227
NBLiHi.

———— Queens County Surrogate Records at Jamaica; abstracts of wills
and administrations, 1787-1835. 1918. 2 vols. (Typed.)   [228
DLC, NBLiHi, NJQ, NN (and microfilm), USlGS.

———— (Inscriptions in) three cemeteries at Sag Harbor and one at
Riverhead, 1773 to 1870. 1911 (*i.e.*, 1912). (Typed.)   [229
Should be three cemeteries; two at Sag Harbor and one at Riverhead: Sag Harbor:
Presbyterian Church cemetery, 1773-1870 (with notes), and cemetery at North
Haven, 1787-1852; new cemetery at Riverhead, 1761-1911.
MnU, NBLiHi, NJQ, NN.

———— Inscriptions from the Methodist cemetery at Searingtown, Nassau County. 1924. (Typed.)   [230
NBLiHi.

———— (Inscriptions in) the First Presbyterian Church cemetery of
Setauket, 1714-1920. (Typed.)   [231
NBLiHi.

———— Southampton town cemetery inscriptions, 1681-1885 (with additional data). (Typed.)   [232
NBLiHi.

———— Springfield, Jamaica, cemetery (inscriptions), 1735 or 1760 to
1909. 1912. (Typed.)   [233
NBLiHi, NJQ, NN.

———— Thoughts and reminiscences of Phebe Smith (Simonson) Higbie of Springfield, Jamaica, New York. 1914. (Typed.)   [234
NBLiHi.

———— Inscriptions from the Tangier Smith burying ground, Strong
Neck. 1921. (Typed.)   [235
NBLiHi.

———— (Inscriptions in) Suffolk County cemeteries, 1754-1923, with
some Bible records and genealogical notes. (Typed.)   [236
Some marriages in Brookhaven, 1799-1847.
Daniel Roe David burying ground at Coram.
Hiram Hulse burying ground, Baiting Hollow, 1857-1861.
Hulse family cemetery, Baiting Hollow, Riverside, 1848-1877.

James Hulse, Muirson, and Punderson family notes.
Hulse and Ruland family notes.
Mount Sinai (Old Mans) Congregational Church cemetery.
Davis burying ground on Hopkins farm, Mt. Sinai, 1790-1851.
Caroline Episcopal Church cemetery, Setauket, 1751-1923.
Setauket Methodist Church cemetery, 1834-1906.
Joseph Brewster burying ground at Strong Neck, 1760-1877.
Old Tangier Smith cemetery at Strong Neck, 1705-1882.
Abstracts from some Suffolk County deeds.
NBLiHi.

———— Suffolk County, New York, Surrogate Records at Riverhead, 1787-1829; Indexes of Wills and Abstracts. Transcribed 1905-1918. 3 vols. [237
DLC, NBLiHi, NJQ, NN (microfilm), USlGS.

———— Genealogical notes on families (of Long Island). (MS collection and microfilm.) [238
NBLiHi.

Earl, Rev. Marmaduke. Marriages on Long Island (Oyster Bay), 1802-1855, performed by the Rev. Marmaduke Earl. Also a typed copy by Josephine C. Frost, 1914. [239
NBLiHi, NJQ, NN.

East Hampton, New York. St. Philomena's Roman Catholic Church. Index to burials in St. Philomena's cemetery. (Typed.) [240
NEh.

———— Records of the Jericho cemetery. Copied 1941. [241
NEh.

Easter, George M(oroni). (Inscriptions in) Rockville cemetery, Lynbrook, New York. 1953. (Typed.) [242
NBLiHi, NJQ, NN (microfilm).

———— The wills of Suffolk County on Long Island in the State of New York. Liber A (1787-1798). Abstracted. 1937. Also liber B, 1798-1809. [243
Liber A: MnH, MWA, NBLiHi, NN; Liber B: NJQ, NN.

Eaton, James Waterbury. History and Records of the First Presbyterian Church of Babylon, New York (1783-1857). Printed by the Church, 1912. (Baptisms, 1798-1857.) [244
DLC, MWA, NBLiHi, NEh, NJQ, NN, NNNGB, NRvS, USlGS.

Eberlein, Harold Donaldson. Manor Houses and Historic Homes of Long Island and Staten Island. 1938. [245
DLC, InU, MBNEH, MiU, N, NBB, NBLiHi, NcRS, NEh, NIC, NJQ, NN, NNC, NNNGB, OCl, ODW, OO, OU, USlGS, ViU.

Edwards, Clarissa. A History of early Sayville. 1935. [246
DLC, DNDAR, MBNEH, N, NBLiHi, NHu, NJQ, NN, NNNGB, NSmB.

Edwards, Sadie and Florence Bryant. Records of the Caroline Episcopal

Church of Setauket, 1822-1930.   (Typed.)   [247
NBLiHi.

Eno, Joel N.   The earliest bouweries in Brooklyn and their owners.   In
New York Geneal. and Biog. Record, 46, pp. 218, 230.   [248
Az, C, CaOTP, CL, CoD, CSf, Ct, CtHi, CtY, DLC, DNDAR, IaHi, IC, ICN, ICU,
In, MB, MBAt, MBNEH, MdBP, MeHi, MH, MHi, Mi, MiD-B, MNF, MnHi, MnM,
MoK, MoS, MWA, N, NB, NBLiHi, NBu, NBuG, Nc, NEh, Nh, NHC, NHi, NIC,
NjNbS, NjPla, NJQ, NN, NNC, NNNGB, NR, OC, OCHP, OCl, OClWHi, OHi,
PEa, PEr, PHi, PPi, PPL, USlGS, Wa, WaS, WM.

Esterbrook, Janet.   First Methodist Episcopal Church of Brooklyn: Records.   Baptisms, 1796-1883; marriages 1802-1886; deaths 1807-1808
and members, 1798-1816.   (Typed.)   [249
NBLiHi.

Evjen, John O.   Scandinavian immigrants in New York, 1630-1674.   1916.
                                                                   [250
DLC, ICJ, MB, MiU, NAu, NBLiHi, NJQ, NN, NNNGB, OCl, PHi, PP, PPLT.

Far Rockaway, New York.   Cornell cemetery at Far Rockaway.   In *Rockaway Review* for December, 1938 (incomplete).   (Mounted clipping.)
NBLiHi.   [251

Far Rockaway, New York, High School.   History of the Rockaways . . .
written by students of Far Rockaway High School, 1932.   [252
DLC, NBLiHi, NEh, NJQ.

Farmingdale, New York.   Cemetery Records.   [253
NEh.

Ferguson, Henry L.   Fisher's Island, New York, 1614-1924.   1925. [254
MWA, N, NN.

Fernow, Berthold, compiler and editor.   Calendar of Wills on file and
recorded in the offices of the Clerk of the Court of Appeals, of the
County Clerk at Albany, and of the Secretary of State 1626-1836.
1896.   [255
CtY, DLC, DNDAR, MBNEH, MH-L, MWA, NBLiHi, NEh, Nh, Nj, NjNbT, NjP,
NJQ, NN, NNNGB, PP, USlGS.

———— Documents relating to the colonial history of the state of New
York.   15 vols.   (especially vol. 14).   [256
DLC, DNDAR, MBNEH, NBLiHi, NEh, NJQ, NN, NNNGB.

———— The (court) records of New Amsterdam from 1653 to 1676.   7
vols.   1897.   [257
This contains many references to Long Island inhabitants.
CU, DLC, MWA, NBLiHi, NEh, Nh, NjNbT, NjP, NJQ, NN, NNNGB, PU-L.

———— New York in the Revolution as Colony and State.   1887-1901.
4 vols.   [258
DLC, MH, NBLiHi, NEh, NN, NNNGB.

Field, Benjamin P(rince).   Babylon reminiscences.   [259
DLC, MWA, N, NBLiHi, NEh, NJQ, NN, NNNGB, NRvS, NSmB.

Fish, John Dean. Hempstead, New York cemetery inscriptions. In *New York Geneal. and Biog. Record, 54,* pp. 201, 335; *55,* pp. 72, 154, 243.
[260
Az, C, CaOTP, CL, CoD, CSf, Ct, CtHi, CtY, DLC, DNDAR, IaHi, IC, ICN, ICU, In, MB, MBAt, MBNEH, MdBP, MeHi, MH, MHi, Mi, MiD-B, MNF, MnHi, MnM, MoK, MoS, MWA, N, NB, NBLiHi, NBu, NBuG, Nc, NEh, Nh, NHC, NHi, NIC, NjNbS, NjPla, NJQ, NN, NNC, NNNGB, NR, OC, OCHP, OCl, OClWHi, OHi, PEa, PEr, PHi, PPi, PPL, USlGS, Wa, WaS, WM.

————— Christ's First Presbyterian Church, Hempstead, New York. Baptisms, 1805-1894; deaths, 1821-1890. 1922. [261
NNNGB.

————— History and Vital Records of Christ's First Presbyterian church of Hempstead, Long Island, New York. In *New York Geneal. and Biog. Record, 53,* pp. 235, 381; *54,* pp. 30, 138. [262
Az, C, CaOTP, CL, CoD, CSf, Ct, CtHi, CtY, DLC, DNDAR, IaHi, IC, ICN, ICU, In, MB, MBAt, MBNEH, MdBP, MeHi, MH, MHi, Mi, MiD-B, MNF, MnHi, MnM, MoK, MoS, MWA, N, NB, NBLiHi, NBu, NBuG, Nc, NEh, Nh, NHC, NHi, NIC, NjNbS, NjPla, NJQ, NN, NNC, NNNGB, NR, OC, OCHP, OCl, OClWHi, OHi, PEa, PEr, PHi, PPi, PPL, USlGS, Wa, WaS, WM.

Flatbush, New York. Inscriptions from the Catholic cemetery, 1863. Transcription. [263
NBLiHi.

————— Deeds and documents relating to Flatbush lands, 1696-1764. [264
NJQ.

————— Flatbush election records, 1799-1894. Includes names of candidates and some poll lists. (MS.) [265
NBLiHi.

————— Inscriptions from the churchyard of the Reformed Dutch Church, 1864. [265a.
NBLiHi.

————— Records of the Reformed Dutch Church of Flatbush, New York. In *Holland Society Year Book,* 1898. [266
DLC, DNDAR, MBNEH, NBLiHi, NEh, NJQ, NN, NNNGB, NNHol, OCl, OClWHi, USlGS.

Flatlands, New York. Flatlands poor accounts, 1809-1830. [267
NBLiHi.

————— Flatlands Reformed Dutch Church burial grounds; inscriptions, 1939. (Typed.) [268
NBLiHi.

————— Flatlands Reformed Dutch Church; miscellaneous records (seventeenth and eighteenth centuries). [269
NBLiHi (microfilm), NjR (microfilm).

Flint, Martha Bockee. Early Long Island — A colonial study. 1896.
[270
DLC, DNW, MBNEH, MnU, N, NB, NBLiHi, NEh, NHu, NIC, NjNbS, NJQ, NN, NNC, NNG, NNNGB, NSmB, OCl, PHi, PP, PPL.

Flushing, New York. Flushing directories: 1880, 1885, 1891, 1895.
NBLiHi. [271

———— Land conveyances in Flushing. 1652-1776.   [272
The originals are in the Bowne House, Flushing, New York.
NN (Manuscript Room).

———— Marriage and birth records, wills and inventories of Flushing.
1677-1783.   [273
The originals are in the Bowne House, Flushing, New York.
NN (Manuscript Room).

———— Flushing Quaker deaths. (Typed.)   [274
NJQ.

———— Flushing Quaker records.   [275
NNNGB (microfilm).

———— Flushing St. George's church. Registers of pew rents, 1837-
1838. (MS.)   [276
NJQ.

———— Society of Friends' Minutes, Flushing Meeting, 1671-1703. [277
NN (Manuscript Room).

Flushing Soldiers' Monument Ass'n. Records. Minutes, 1865 (record of
soldiers from Flushing serving in the Civil War). 2 vols. (MS.) [278
NJQ.

Flushing, Town of. Town Records of Flushing, 1790-1885. Vols. 1, 2, 3.
The earlier town records have been destroyed.   [279
NJQ, NNNGB (microfilm of vols. 1, 2).

Forbush, William Byron. Wantagh, Jerusalem and Ridgewood, 1644-1892;
a historical sketch. 1892.   [280
NBLiHi, NN, NSmB.

Force, Peter. Census (heads of families), July, 1776, for Brookhaven,
East Hampton, Islip, Manor of St. George and the Patentship of Merit-
ches (Moriches), Shelter Island, Smithtown, Southampton, Southold.
In *American Archives*, 4th Series, vol. 6, cols. 1236-1252.   [281
AU, CaT, CoU, DLC, DN, DNLM, MBAt, MdBP, MnH, NBLiHi, NcD, NEh, Nh,
NjN, NjP, NN, NNNGB, OU.

Fowler, Ida. History of Little Neck. 1952.   [282
NJQ, NN.

Freeport, New York. Cemetery Records of Freeport   [283
NNNGB (microfilm).

Frost, Josephine C. Gravestone inscriptions of Astoria, Long Island,
1788-1845. (MS.)   [284
NNNGB.

———— Brooklyn, New York. Records of St. Ann's (Episcopal) Church.
Baptisms, 1780-1870; marriages 1793-1870; deaths 1798-1866; communicants from 1788, and genealogical extracts from the first two
minute books, 1774-1828. 5 vols. (Typed.)   [285
NBLiHi, NN (microfilm), NNNGB.

———— Brooklyn, New York. Genealogical gleanings from book 2 of conveyances, Kings County. In *New York Geneal. and Biog. Record,* *54,* 105-111, 241-251, 303-319.   [286
Az, C, CaOTP, CL, CoD, CSf, Ct, CtHi, CtY, DLC, DNDAR, IaHi, IC, ICN, ICU, In, MB, MBAt, MBNEH, MdBP, MeHi, MH, MHi, Mi, MiD-B, MNF, MnHi, MnM, MoK, MoS, MWA, N, NB, NBLiHi, NBu, NBuG, Nc, NEh, Nh, NHC, NHi, NIC, NjNbS, NjPla, NJQ, NN, NNC, NNNGB, NR, OC, OCHP, OCl, OClWHi, OHi, PEa, PEr, PHi, PPi, PPL, USlGS, Wa, WaS, WM.

———— Inscriptions from the Flatbush Protestant Dutch Reformed Church graveyard. 1921. (Typed.)   [287
NBLiHi, NN, NNNGB.

———— Flatbush Protestant Dutch Reformed Church records. Baptisms, 1677-1872; marriages 1677-1866; members 1677-1872; and miscellaneous, 1677-1872. 5 vols. (Typed.)   [288
MBNEH, NBLiHi, NNNGB.

———— Flushing Monthly Meeting, Marriage Certificates, 1663 to . . . (Copy of Record Book No. 213). (Typed.)   [289
NNNGB.

———— Flushing Quaker Records, 1660-1840. (Typed.)   [290
NNNGB.

———— Genealogical gleanings from the town records of Gravesend. (MS.)   [291
NBLiHi.

———— Cemetery Inscriptions from Hempstead, Long Island, New York. Copied 191—. (Typed.)   [292
DLC, NJQ, NN, NNNGB.

———— Record of Baptisms in Christ's First Presbyterian Church of Hempstead, Long Island (New York), 1805-1894. (Typed.)   293
NNNGB.

———— St. George's Episcopal Church records, Hempstead, New York. Marriages, 1786-1845. Births and Deaths, 1725-1847. (Typed.)   [294
MBNEH, NBLiHi, NNNGB.

———— Cemetery Inscriptions from Huntington, Long Island, New York. Copied 1911. (Typed.)   [295
DLC, MBNEH, NBLiHi, NJQ, NNNGB.

———— Jamaica, New York. Cemetery inscriptions at Black Stump adjoining John Eisman's Farm, and the Van Wicklen cemetery. In *Long Island Cemetery Inscriptions,* vol. 1, p. 1.   [296
MBNEH, NBLiHi, NN.

———— Baptismal Records of the First Reformed Dutch Church at Jamaica, New York, 1702-1851. 4 vols. 1912-1913. (Typed.)   [297
DLC, DNDAR, MBNEH, NBLiHi, NJQ, NNNGB, USlGS.

———— Marriages at Jamaica, New York, First Reformed Dutch Church, 1803-1851. 1913. (Typed.)   [298
DLC, NBLiHi, NJQ, NNNGB, USlGS.

———— Jamaica, Long Island Town Records, 1656-1751 (*i.e.,* 1753), 3 vols. Edited by Josephine C. Frost, 1914.   [299
DLC, DNDAR, MB, MBNEH, MH, MWA, N, NB, NBLiHi, NEh, NHu, NJQ, NN, NNNGB, USlGS.

———— Jericho, Long Island Monthly Meeting (Quaker Records), Hempstead. Births, 1812-1887; Marriages, 1790-1900; Deaths, 1813-1888. (Typed.)   [300
DLC, NJQ, NN, NNNGB.

———— Long Island Cemeteries. *Also titled* Long Island Cemetery Inscriptions. (Typed.)   [301

Cataloging varies in different libraries, some from either of the foregoing, or by individual locations.

(This listing from the Queens Borough Public Library.)

AQUEDUCT: Southside cemetery (Van Wicklen), I, pp. 25-28.

BAYSIDE: Lawrence cemetery, I, pp. 34-36.

BAYVILLE: Cemetery (four miles northeast of Locust Valley station), III, pp. 42-49.

BROOKLYN: Reformed Dutch churchyard (Flatbush), XI, pp. 57-99; Flatlands cemetery, XII, pp. 1-52; Gravesend cemetery, XI, pp. 1-56; New Lotts *(sic)* cemetery, IX, pp. 21-33, 34-53.

COLD SPRING: Whitney cemetery (Fountain Hill cemetery), II, pp. 41-45.

COLD SPRING HARBOR: St. John's Church cemetery, XII, pp. 53-60.

EAST NORWICH: Locust cemetery, originally Duryea cemetery, I, pp. 43-45; Old cemetery, I, pp. 40-42, 46.

ELMHURST: Newtown cemetery on Old Court St., XII, pp. 86-99.

ELWOOD: *Blackly (sic:* Blachley) cemetery, XII, p. 73.

FLATBUSH: see Brooklyn.

FLATLANDS: see Brooklyn.

FLOWER HILL: Old cemetery, II, p. 27.

FLUSHING: Parsons cemetery, IX, pp. 18-20; Quaker cemetery, V, pp. 14-20; St. George's Episcopal churchyard, IV, pp. 78-95.

FREEPORT: Powell cemetery (1½ miles northeast of Freeport), I, p. 33.

GLEN COVE: Coles cemetery, III, pp. 15-16; Episcopal cemetery, III, pp. 19-41; Old cemetery, II, pp. 96-98; III, p. 17; Townsend cemetery, II, pp. 91-95; Woolsey cemetery, I, pp. 3-5; Wright cemetery, III, p. 18.

GLEN HEAD: Brookville cemetery, I, pp. 47-91; Jotham Townsend cemetery, III, p. 52; Townsend cemetery, III, pp. 50-51.

GRAVESEND: see Brooklyn.

GREAT NECK: Allen cemetery, II, p. 18; old cemeteries, II, pp. 15-17; Treadwell cemetery, II, pp. 19-21.

GREENVALE: Hillside cemetery (near Glen Head station), III, pp. 53-79.

HEMPSTEAD: Methodist churchyard, XVIII, pp. 52-61; Presbyterian churchyard, XVIII, pp. 62-91; private cemetery east of park on Fulton St., XVIII, pp. 41-51; St. George's Episcopal churchyard, XX, pp. 1-82; Town cemetery, XVIII, pp. 1-40.

HICKSVILLE: Schenck cemetery (two miles from Hicksville on Syosset road), II, p. 13.

HOPEDALE: Remsen cemetery (Trotting Course Lane near Williamsburg Road), I, p. 6.

HUNTINGTON: First cemetery, XVI, pp. 1-87.

JAMAICA: Brinckerhoff cemetery, I, pp. 1-2; Grace Episcopal churchyard, XV, pp. 9-76; Lott family cemetery, IX, pp. 1-17; Methodist cemetery, XV, pp. 1-8; Prospect cemetery, XIV, pp. 1-137 (NJQ has additions).

JERICHO: Lewis cemetery, II, p. 14; Quaker cemetery, V, pp. 21-39.

KINGS PARK: Cemetery on property of Kings Park State Hospital, west of the powerhouse near the canal, XII, pp. 64-65; Old cemetery southeast of Kings Park State Hospital, XII, pp. 67-68; Vail cemetery, XII, p. 66.

LATTINGTOWN: Latting cemetery, III, p. 14.

LAWRENCE: Old cemetery, I, p. 29.

LITTLE NECK: Zion churchyard, VI, pp. 56-80.

LOCUST VALLEY: Cock cemetery, XVII, p. 12; Frost cemetery, XVII, pp. 17-25; Tilley cemetery, III, pp. 12-13; Weekes cemetery, XVII, pp. 14-16.

MANHASSET: Episcopal and Dutch Reformed churchyard, XIX, pp. 1-99; Quaker cemetery, V, pp. 1-13.

MATINECOCK: Friends' cemetery, XVII, pp. 27-42; Peacock Point cemetery, XVII, p. 13.

MATTITUCK: Old part of cemetery, VII, pp. 41-88.

MEADOW BROOK: Small cemetery, I, p. 9; Smith cemetery, I, p. 8.

MILL NECK: Cocks cemetery, II, pp. 88-90.

MUTTONTOWN: Weekes cemetery, XII, pp. 75-76.

NEW LOTTS: see Brooklyn.

NEWTOWN: Betts cemetery (Penny Bridge Road near Betts Ave.), I, pp. 30-31; Cumberson cemetery (Betts Ave. cor. Thomson Ave.), I, p. 32; Dutch Reformed cemetery, IV, pp. 1-24; Folk cemetery (Train's Meadow Road), I, p. 7; Gorsline cemetery, I, p. 10; Presbyterian cemetery, IV, pp. 44-75; St. James Episcopal cemetery, IV, pp. 25-43.

NEW UTRECHT: St. John's Lutheran cemetery, IX, pp. 54-120.

NORTH BEACH: Riker cemetery, XII, pp. 80-85d.

OYSTER BAY: Adams cemetery, XII, p. 74; Albertson cemetery, II, pp. 46-52; Smith cemetery (Cove Neck), II, p. 61; Fleet cemetery (two miles southeast of Oyster Bay village), II, pp. 62-64; Fort Hill cemetery, XII, pp. 77-79; Larrabee and White cemeteries, II, pp. 56-59; McCoun cemetery, II, pp. 53-55; Old cemetery, I, p. 46; Presbyterian churchyard, II, p. 60; Reformed churchyard, III, pp. 1-11; Underhill cemetery, XVII, pp. 1-11; Wortman cemetery, I, pp. 11-12; Youngs cemetery, II, pp. 65-77.

PORT WASHINGTON: Cornwell cemetery, II, pp. 24-26; Hegeman-Onderdonk cemetery (also called Flower Hill cemetery), II, pp. 29-40; Old cemetery, II, p. 23; Mitchell cemetery, II, p. 28; Sands cemetery, II, p. 22.

RICHMOND HILL: Wyckoff-Snedeker cemetery, I, pp. 13-24.

RIVERHEAD: Town cemetery, X, pp. 1-154.

ROCKAWAY: Cornell cemetery, IV, pp. 76-77.

SANDS POINT: Sands cemetery, II, pp. 1-8.

SETAUKET: Brewster cemetery, XII, pp. 69-72.

SMITHTOWN: Cemetery overlooking the bay, XII, pp. 61-63.

SOUTHOLD: Presbyterian cemetery, XIII, pp. 1-175; Willow Hill cemetery, XIII, pp. 176-230.

SYOSSET: Cheshire cemetery, II, p. 9, Memorial cemetery (two miles northeast of Syosset), II, pp. 78-87; Schenck cemetery, II, pp. 10-12.

WADING RIVER: Hulse cemetery, VII, pp. 1-38.

WESTBURY: Quaker cemetery, VI, pp. 1-55.

WHEATLEY: Old cemetery, I, pp. 92-94.

WOODSIDE: Moore cemetery (Bowery Bay Road), I, pp. 37-39.

MBNEH, NBLiHi, NJQ (13 vols.), N (bound as 14 vols.), NNNGB (13 vols.).

———— Baptisms: New Utrecht, 1718-1741; Flatlands, 1747-1775. (Dutch Reformed churches.) (Typed.) [302

NBLiHi, NNNGB.

———— Cemetery Inscriptions (Oyster Bay, New York). The Fort Hill Cemetery, and the Wortman cemetery on Underhill property. In *Long Island Hist. Soc. Quarterly, 2*, pp. 50-52. [303

CoD, Ct, CtY, CU, DLC, DSI-M, ICN, IU, MeU, MH, MHi, MiD-B, MnHi, MWA, N, NB, NBB, NBLiHi, NBP, NBuG, NEh, NjP, NJQ, NN, NNC, OHi, PCA, PHi, VW, WaU, WHi.

———— Baptismal record of the Reformed Dutch Church at Oyster Bay, Long Island, New York, 1741-1846. Marriages, 1826-1847. 1913. (Typed.) [304

DLC, NJQ, NNNGB, USlGS.

———— Dutch Reformed Church records, Wolver Hollow, Oyster Bay, New York. In *New York Geneal. and Biog. Record, 73*, pp. 26, 121, 200, 273. [305

Az, C, CaOTP, CL, CoD, CSf, Ct, CtHi, CtY, DLC, DNDAR, IaHi, IC, ICN, ICU, In, MB, MBAt, MBNEH, MdBP, MeHi, MH, MHi, Mi, MiD-B, MNF, MnHi, MnM, MoK, MoS, MWA, N, NB, NBLiHi, NBu, NBuG, Nc, NEh, Nh, NHC, NHi, NIC, NjNbS, NjPla, NJQ, NN, NNC, NNNGB, NR, OC, OCHP, OCl, OClWHi, OHi, PEa, PEr, PHi, PPi, PPL, USlGS, Wa, WaS, WM.

———— Riverhead tombstone inscriptions. (Typed.)   [306

From the town cemetery, and from stones removed there from the Methodist and Swedenborgian cemeteries.
NBLiHi, NN, NNNGB.

———— Vital records from the *Corrector* for 1854 (Sag Harbor). (MS.)
NNNGB.   [307

———— Cemetery inscriptions of Smithtown, Long Island, 1770-1885.
(MS.)   [308
NNNGB.

———— Notes from Town Records of Southold, Long Island, not in printed books. (MS.)   [309
NNNGB.

Frost, Josephine C., et al. Vital records from the *Long Island Star* and *Brooklyn Evening Star*, 1809-1846. (To be continued to 1863.) On cards; 108 drawers.   [310
NBLiHi.

Fulton, Henry. Farm line map of the city of Brooklyn from official records and surveys, compiled and drawn by Henry Fulton. 1874.   [311
NB, NBLiHi, NJQ, NN.

Furman, Gabriel. Notes, geographical and historical, relating to the town of Brooklyn. 1824.   [312
DLC, NEh, NNHi, NBLiHi (and original MS), NN.

———— Notes, geographical and historical, relating to the town of Brooklyn. Reprinted in 1865.   [313
DLC, MBAt, MH, MiU-C, MnH, MnU, MWA, N, NB, NBC, NBuG, NBLiHi, NIC, NJQ, NN, NNC, NNNGB, NSmB, ODW, PBL, PPPrHi.

Gardiner, David. Chronicles of the Town of Easthampton [!], county of Suffolk, New York. 1871.   [314
DLC, MWA, N, NBLiHi, NEh, NHuHi, NJQ, NN, NNNGB, NSmB.

Gardiner, John Lyon. Notes and observations on the town of East Hampton … 1798. In *Coll. of the New York Hist. Soc.*, 1869, pp. 225ff. [315
DLC, NBLiHi, NEh, NJQ, NN.

Gardiner, Sarah Diodati. Early Memories of Gardiner's Island (the Isle of Wight), New York. Chronology by Abigail Fithian Halsey. 1947.
DLC, DNDAR, NBLiHi, NEh, NJQ, NN, NNNGB.   [316

Gardner, Charles Carroll. Census of Newtown, Long Island, August, 1698.
In *The American Genealogist, 24*, pp. 133-137.   [317
CL, CoD, Ct, CtHi, CtY, DLC, DNGS, ICN, In, KHi, MB, MPB, MWA, MeBa, MeHi, Mi, MiD-B, MnHi, MoS, N, NBuG, NN, NJQ, NR, OC, OCHP, OCl, OClWHi, OHi, PEr, PHi, VW, WHi, WaSp.

Gateley's Directories. Gateley's directory of Bay Shore and Brightwaters, Long Island, New York. 1929.   [318
NJQ.

Gravesend, New York. Gravesend assessment roll, 1799, 1877-1880. (MS.) [319
NBLiHi.

Greene, Rev. Zachariah. Marriages performed at Cutchogue, 1787-1797; marriages, 1797-1848, and deaths, 1797-1845, at Setauket. (MS.) [320
NBLiHi.

Griffin, Augustus. Diaries of Augustus Griffin: June, 1792-1850. [321
NBLiHi (original); NJQ (June, 1792-September 1800; 1800-1822; 1833-1839).

———— Griffin's Journal. First Settlers of Southold; the names of the heads of those families being only thirteen at the time of their landing. 1857. [322
CU, DLC, MBNEH, N, NB, NBLiHi, NcU, NEh, NJQ, NN, NNNGB, NSmB, USIGS.

———— Records of marriages, 1677-1859, and deaths, 1696-1861, in Southold, Shelter Island and other parts of the state of New York. Typed by Frances E. Willcox. [323
NBLiHi (original and typed copy).

Griffin, Walter Kenneth. Baptisms, Dutch church at New Utrecht, New York. In *New York Geneal. and Biog. Record*, *73*, p. 96. [324
Az, C, CaOTP, CL, CoD, CSf, Ct, CtHi, CtY, DLC, DNDAR, IaHi, IC, ICN, ICU, In, MB, MBAt, MBNEH, MdBP, MeHi, MH, MHi, Mi, MiD-B, MNF, MnHi, MnM, MoK, MoS, MWA, N, NB, NBLiHi, NBu, NBuG, Nc, NEh, Nh, NHC, NHi, NIC, NjNbS, NjPla, NJQ, NN, NNC, NNNGB, NR, OC, OCHP, OCl, OClWHi, OHi, PEa, PEr, PHi, PPi, PPL, USIGS, Wa, WaS, WM.

Gritman, Charles T. Jamaica, Long Island . . . A Documentary History of Jamaica, L. I., 1655-1800. [325
Vol 1 only: contains also marriages performed by the Rev. Marmaduke Earl, 1793-1835.
NN.

———— Historical Miscellany. 4 vols. (MS.) [326
Notes chiefly from New York state, including Long Island.
NN.

———— A register of the inhabitants of Jamaica, Queens County, L. I., 1656-1710. (Typed.) [327
NN, NNNGB.

———— An index of land records of Queens County, A to H only. 1920. (Typed.) [328
NN, NNNGB.

———— Genealogical data of many families . . . with supplement. 3 vols. (MS.) [329
NN.

Haight, John Sylvanus. Adventures for God. [330
Includes a transcript from the records of St. George's Episcopal church, Hempstead, New York.
DLC, DNDAR, MBNEH, MWA, NBLiHi, NEh, NJQ, NN, NNNGB, NSmB, USIGS.

Harris, Edward Doubleday. Ancient Long Island Epitaphs. 8 vols.

(MS.) [331

Cemetery inscriptions are reported for Amagansett, Amityville, Aquebogue, Astoria, Bridgehampton, Brookhaven, Cutchogue, East Hampton, Jamesport, Mattituck, Melville (Lower), Mount Sinai, New Utrecht, Riverhead, Sag Harbor, Setauket, Shelter Island, Smithtown, Southampton, South Haven, Southold, Westhampton. NNNGB.

———— Amagansett, New York, cemetery inscriptions. In *New Eng. Hist. Geneal. Register, 54,* pp. 61-62, 203-205. [332

Az, C, CL, CoD, CSt, Ct, CtHi, CtHT, CtY, CU, DCU, DLC, DNDAR, GA, GHi, ICN, ICU, In, InI, IU, KHi, KyLoF, M, MB, MBAt, MBC, MBNEH, MdBE, MdBP, Me, MeB, MeBa, MeHi, MeP, MH, MHi, Mi, MiD-B, MiGr, MiMu, MiU, MiU-C, MNF, MnHi, MoK, MoS, MPB, MWA, MWiW, N, NBLiHi, NbO, NBu, Nc, NEh, NhD, NHi, NIC, NjP, NjPla, NJQ, NjR, NN, NNC, NNNGB, NNS, NNU-H, NR, OC, OCHP, OCl, OClWHi, OHi, OMC, OrP, PEa, PEr, PHi, PPi, PPL, PWb, RP, TC, Tx, USlGS, Vi, Wa, WaS, WHi, WH.

———— East Hampton, New York, cemetery inscriptions. In *New Eng. Hist. Geneal. Register, 54,* pp. 205-210, 301-308, 427-434; *55,* pp. 84, 278. [333

Az, C, CL, CoD, CSt, Ct, CtHi, CtHT, CtY, CU, DCU, DLC, DNDAR, GA, GHi, ICN, ICU, In, InI, IU, KHi, KyLoF, M, MB, MBAt, MBC, MBNEH, MdBE, MdBP, Me, MeB, MeBa, MeHi, MeP, MH, MHi, Mi, MiD-B, MiGr, MiMu, MiU, MiU-C, MNF, MnHi, MoK, MoS, MPB, MWA, MWiW, N, NBLiHi, NbO, NBu, Nc, NEh, NhD, NHi, NIC, NjP, NjPla, NJQ, NjR, NN, NNC, NNNGB, NNS, NNU-H, NR, OC, OCHP, OCl, OClWHi, OHi, OMC, OrP, PEa, PEr, PHi, PPi, PPL, PWb, RP, T, TC, Tx, USlGS, Vi, Wa, WaS, WHi, WM.

———— Some of ye older Epitaphs in ye public burial place of Huntington, 1906. [334

NBLiHi, NEh, NNNGB.

———— Inscriptions from the cemetery in Orient, L. I., in *Ancient Long Island Epitaphs,* with genealogical notes by Lucy D. Akerly. [335

MBNEH, NBLiHi, NN, NNNGB.

———— Shelter Island, New York, gravestone inscriptions. In *New Eng. Hist. Geneal. Register, 54,* p. 53. [336

Az, C, CL, CoD, CSt, Ct, CtHi, CtHT, CtY, CU, DCU, DLC, DNDAR, GA, GHi, ICN, ICU, In, InI, IU, KHi, KyLoF, M, MB, MBAt. MBC, MBNEH, MdBE, MdBP, Me, MeB, MeBa, MeHi, MeP, MH, MHi, Mi, MiD-B, MiGr, MiMu, MiU, MiU-C, MNF, MnHi, MoK, MoS, MPB, MWA, MWiW, N, NBLiHi, NbO, NBu, Nc, NEh, NhD, NHi, NIC, NjP, NjPla, NJQ, NjR, NN, NNC. NNNGB, NNS, NNU-H. NR. OC, OCHP, OCl, OClWHi, OHi, OMC, OrP, PEa, PEr, PHi, PPi, PPL, PWb, RP, T, TC, Tx, USlGS, Vi, Wa, WaS, WHi, WM.

———— Southold, New York, First Church: gravestone inscriptions. In *New Eng. Hist. Geneal. Register, 53,* pp. 74, 169, 325, 413. [337

Az, C, CL, CoD, CSt, Ct, CtHi, CtHT, CtY, CU, DCU, DLC, DNDAR, GA, GHI, ICN, ICU, In, InI, IU, KHi, KyLoF, M, MB, MBAt, MBC, MBNEH, MdBE, MdBP, Me, MeB, MeBa, MeHi, MeP, MH, MHi, Mi, MiD-B, MiGr, MiMu, MiU. MiU-C, MNF, MnHi, MoK, MoS, MPB, MWA, MWiW, N, NBLiHi, NbO, NBu, Nc, NEh, NhD, NHi, NIC, NjP, NjPla, NJQ, NjR, NN, NNC, NNNGB, NNS, NNU-H, NR, OC, OCHP, OCl, OClWHi, OHi, OMC, OrP, PEa, PEr, PHi, PPi, PPL, PWb, RP, T, TC, Tx, USlGS, Vi, Wa, WaS, WHi, WM.

———— Ancient Long Island epitaphs from the towns of Southold, Shelter Island and Easthampton [!], New York. 1903. [338

Includes East Hampton wills, 1665-1786, transcribed by Orville B. Ackerly.

DLC, DNDAR, ICN, MBNEH, N, NBLiHi, NEh, NJQ, NN, NNNGB, PHi, USlGS.

———— Wainscott, New York, cemetery inscriptions. In *New Eng. Hist. Geneal. Register, 54,* pp. 278-279. [339

Az, C, CL, CoD, CSt, Ct, CtHi, CtHT, CtY, CU, DCU, DLC, DNDAR, GA, GHi, ICN,

ICU, In, InI, IU, KHi, KyLoF, M, MB, MBAt, MBC, MBNEH, MdBE, MdBP, Me, MeB, MeBa, MeHi, MeP, MH, MHi, Mi, MiD-B, MiGr, MiMu, MiU, MiU-C, MNF, MnHi, MoK, MoS, MPB, MWA, MWiW, N, NBLiHi, NbO, NBu, Nc, NEh, NhD, NHi, NIC, NjP, NjPla, NJQ, NjR, NN, NNC, NNNGB, NNS, NNU-H, NR, OC, OCHP, OCl, OClWHi, OHi, OMC, OrP, PEa, PEr, PHi, PPi, PPL, PWb, RP, T, TC, Tx, USlGS, Vi, Wa, WaS, WHi, WM.

Hauxhurst, James. Journal and account book of James Hauxhurst of Flushing and Oyster Bay, 1797-1851. [340
NN (Manuscript Room).

Haviland, Frank. Friends' cemetery in Prospect Park, Brooklyn, New York. (1) Copy of the original register of interments to 1906; (2) Inscriptions. 1906. [341
MBNEH, NBLiHi.

———— Zion Episcopal churchyard inscriptions, Douglaston, Long Island. 1904. (Typed.) [342
NBLiHi.

———— Flushing Friends' Monthly Meeting. Births. 1640-1796. (Typed.) [343
NBLiHi.

———— Flushing Friends' Monthly Meeting. Births, 1801-1880, including some earlier; marriages 1806-1878, complete; deaths 1801-1880, including some earlier. (Typed.) [344
NBLiHi.

———— Flushing Friends' Monthly Meeting. Marriages, 1764-1821. (Typed.) [345
NBLiHi.

———— Flushing Friends' Monthly Meeting. Marriage Certificates, 1663-1822. (Typed.) [346
NNNGB.

———— Flushing Friends' Monthly Meeting. Records from Isaac Horner's book, 1669-1796. (Typed.) [347
NBLiHi.

———— Flushing Friends' Monthly Meeting. Removal Certificates, 1805-1877. (Typed.) [348
NBLiHi.

———— Jericho Friends' records: births 1812-1887; deaths, 1813-1888; marriages 1790-1900; members from Samuel J. Underhill's book (19th century); cemetery. (Typed.) [349
NBLiHi.

———— Quaker Tombstones of Long Island, New York. 1904. (Typed.) Inscriptions from Flushing, Jericho, Manhasset, Matinecock, and Westbury. [350
MBNEH, NBLiHi, NN, NNNGB.

———— Inscriptions from . . . Methodist churchyard, the Town cemetery (graded over 1897), the cemetery back of the Presbyterian church, and a private burying ground, Hempstead (New York). 1904. (Typed.) [351
MBNEH, NBLiHi.

———— Private burying ground next the Presbyterian manse, Hempstead. 1904. (Typed.) [352

All but 4 stones were gone by 1949.
NBLiHi.

———— All inscriptions from the Friends' Burying Ground at Manhasset. 1904. (Typed.) [353
NBLiHi.

———— Complete inscriptions from the churchyard of the Dutch Reformed Church of Newtown. 1904. (Typed.) [354
NBLiHi.

———— All inscriptions in the Presbyterian churchyard, Newtown. 1904. (Typed.) [355
NBLiHi.

———— Complete inscriptions from the churchyard of St. James Episcopal Church, Newtown. 1904. (Typed.) [356
NBLiHi.

Hazelton, Henry Isham. The Boroughs of Brooklyn and Queens, counties of Nassau and Suffolk, Long Island, New York, 1609-1924. 1925. [357
DLC, DNDAR, MBNEH, MWA, NB, NBB, NBLiHi, NEh, NHu, NJQ, NN, NNNGB, PHi, USIGS.

Hedges, Henry P(arsons). A centennial and historical address delivered at Bridgehampton, July 4, 1876. [358
This refers to soldiers and sailors who served in the Civil War, born in or enlisted from Bridgehampton.
NBLiHi, NJQ, NN, NNNGB.

———— Bridgehampton, New York, Presbyterian church. Officers of the church. Resident communicants. 1886. [359
DLC, MH, NB, NBLiHi, NJQ, NN, NSmB.

———— Address . . . 200th anniversary of settlement of the town of East Hampton, 1850. [360
Family history and census of 1683.
NBLiHi, NJQ, NN.

———— A History of the Town of East Hampton, New York. With appendix and genealogical notes. 1897. [361
CU, DLC, DNDAR, MBNEH, MdBP, MWA, N, NBLiHi, NEh, NHu, NHuHi, NjP, NJQ, NN, NNC, NNNGB, NRvS, NSmB, USIGS.

———— Records of the Town of East Hampton, New York, edited by Henry P. Hedges (et al), and published by the town. 1887-1905. 6 vols. (Town Records) plus 9 vols. (Trustees Records.) [362
The early records of the First Church are in the back of vol. 5.
DLC, DNDAR, MB, MBNEH, MH, NBLiHi, NEh, Nh, NjP, NJQ, NN, NNNGB, OU, PBL, USIGS.

Hegeman, John. Marriages from records kept by Mr. John Hegeman, 1754-1844. [363
This constitutes part of No. 201.
NJQ, NN.

———— Some of the marriages from the records kept by Mr. John Hege-

man of the town of Oyster Bay . . . 1776-1835. (Typed.)   [364
NBLiHi.

Hegeman, Thomas. Court Records of Thomas Hegeman, Justice of the
Peace of New Utrecht, 1821-1828. (MS.)   [365
NBLiHi.

Heiser, Evelyn M. Cemetery lot-holders and interments for 1862-1868,
Flushing. From newspapers.   [366
NBLiHi.

———— Inscriptions from cemeteries in Newtown, from newspaper clippings of 1880. 1940. Dutch Reformed, Fish-Luyster, and Alsop family
cemeteries. (Typed.)   [367
NBLiHi.

Hempstead, New York. Account books of the Onderdonk paper mill at
Hempstead, 1785-1810. (MS.)   [368
NHi.

———— Hempstead local papers, 1731-1822. 1 folder.   [369
NHi.

———— St. George's Episcopal Church. Marriages from records of the
church. (MS.)   [370
NEh, NNNGB (microfilm).

Henshaw, William W. Encyclopaedia of American Quaker Genealogy.
Vol. 3 (New York).   [371
DLC, DNDAR, MBNEH, NBLiHi, NJQ, NN, NNNGB, USlGS.

Hewlett, New York. Trinity Episcopal Church of Hewlett; excerpts of
burial records, 1845.   [372
NBLiHi.

Hicks, Benjamin D(oughty). Records of St. George's Episcopal Church,
Hempstead, New York. In *New York Geneal. and Biog. Record, 9*, p.
182; *10*, pp. 16, 89, 133; *11*, pp. 47, 88, 133; *12*, pp. 45, 78, 141; *13*, pp.
93, 140; *14*, pp. 43, 70, 116; *15*, pp. 77, 111, 176; and *24*, p. 79.   [373
Az, C, CaOTP, CL, CoD, CSf, Ct, CtHi, CtY, DLC, DNDAR, IaHi, IC, ICN, ICU,
In, MB, MBAt, MBNEH, MdBP, MeHi, MH, MHi, Mi, MiD-B, MNF, MnHi, MnM,
MoK, MoS, MWA, N, NB, NBLiHi, NBu, NBuG, Nc, NEh, Nh, NHC, NHi, NIC,
NjNbS, NjPla, NJQ, NN, NNC, NNNGB, NR, OC, OCHP, OCl, OClWHi, OHi,
PEa, PEr, PHi, PPi, PPL, USlGS, Wa, WaS, WM.

———— Records of the towns of North and South Hempstead, Long Island (1654-1895). 8 vols. 1896-1904.   [374
DLC, NBLiHi, NN, NNNGB.

———— Records of the Society of Friends of Westbury. In *New York
Geneal. and Biog. Record, 16*, p. 171; *17*, p. 218.   [375
Az, C, CaOTP, CL, CoD, CSf, Ct, CtHi, CtY, DLC, DNDAR, IaHi, IC, ICN, ICU,
In, MB, MBAt, MBNEH, MdBP, MeHi, MH, MHi, Mi, MiD-B, MNF, MnHi, MnM,
MoK, MoS, MWA, N, NB, NBLiHi, NBu, NBuG, Nc, NEh, Nh, NHC, NHi, NIC,
NjNbS, NjPla, NJQ, NN, NNC, NNNGB, NR, OC, OCHP, OCl, OClWHi, OHi,
PEa, PEr, PHi, PPi, PPL, USlGS, Wa, WaS, WM.

————— Long Island families; from the manuscripts of the late Benjamin Doughty Hicks of Old Westbury. Transcribed by Florence E. Youngs. [376

NBLiHi.

Hill, George and Frank H. Hill. Account books of the undertaking business of George and Frank H. Hill at Riverhead, New York, 1859-1890. 4 vols. (MS.) [377

NBLiHi.

Hillman, E. Haviland. List of the principal freeholders of Queens County who congratulated Lord Cornbury on his safe arrival in New York May 3, 1702. Copied from the original in the Public Record Office, London, 1915. (MS.) [378

NNNGB.

Hinman, R. R. A Catalogue of the names of the early Puritan settlers of the colony of Connecticut. 1852. [379

Includes the names of settlers who removed to Long Island.
DLC, MBC, MBNEH, MdBJ, MdBP, MiU-C, MnH, NBLiHi, Nh, NIC, NjNbS, NjP, NN, NNNGB, OCl, OClWHi, OO, OOxM, PHi, PPPrHi.

Historical Records Survey. See United States Government Works Progress Administration; Historical Records Survey, Nos. 771, 772, 773, 773a, 774, and 775.

Hoadley, Charles J. Records of the colony and plantation of New Haven, 1638-1649. [380

Includes records of Long Islanders at that time under the jurisdiction of New Haven.
DLC, MA, MB, MBNEH, MdBP, NBLiHi, NjP, NjR, NN, NNNGB.

————— Records of the colony or jurisdiction of New Haven, 1653-1664.
DLC, MA, MB, MBNEH, MdBP, NBLiHi, NjP, NjR, NN, NNNGB. [381

Homan, L. Beecher. Yaphank as it is, and was, and will be . . . 1875.
DLC, MBNEH, N, NBLiHi, NEh, NHu, NJQ, NN, NSmB. [382

Hopkins, Griffith Morgan. Detailed estate and old farm line atlas of the city of Brooklyn, from official records, private plans and actual surveys, based upon the plans deposited in the Assessor's office. 1880. [383

DLC, NB, NBLiHi.

Horner, Isaac. Flushing, New York. Catalogue of the birth of Friends' children. (Typed.) [384

NJQ.

Horton, Jonathan. A census of Baiting Hollow parish by families, Jan. 1, 1825 (with notes by James F. Young). 1906. [385

N, NBLiHi, NJQ, NN, NSmB.

Horton, S. Wentworth. Southold town, Suffolk County, New York—with

genealogies of the founding families, by Wayland Jefferson. 1938. [386
DLC, NBLiHi, NN, NNNGB.

Howell, George Rogers. New York province. Supplementary list of marriage licenses. 1898. [387
DLC, MBNEH, NBLiHi, NEh, NN, NNNGB.

———— The Early History of Southampton, L. I., with Genealogies.
First edition, 1866; second, 1887. [388
DLC [1,2], DNDAR [2], MBNEH [1,2], MnHi [1,2], MnU [1,2] MWA [1,2], N [1,2], NBLiHi [1,2], NEh [1,2],
NHu [2], NjP [2], NJQ [1,2], NN [1,2], NNNGB [1,1], NSmB [1,2], OClWHi [1,2], PHi [1,2], PPPrHi [1,2].
(Superscripts refer to editions)

———— Southampton vital records. (MS.) [389
Mostly used in his *Early History of Southampton, L. I.* 1887.
NBLiHi.

Huntington, Edna. Arshamomaque cemetery inscriptions. 1941. (Typed.)
NBLiHi. [390

———— Brooklyn assessment book, 1810. (Typed.) [391
NBLiHi.

———— Brooklyn deaths, 1806-1848, from the city directory for 1848-
1849. (Typed.) [392
NBLiHi.

———— Brooklyn marriages, 1847, from the city register for 1848.
(Typed.) [393
NBLiHi.

———— Brooklyn marriages and deaths, from the *Long Island Patriot,*
1821-1833. (Typed.) [394
NBLiHi.

———— Brooklyn marriages and deaths from miscellaneous newspapers
published in Brooklyn, 1800-1886. 2 vols. (Typed.) [395
NBLiHi.

———— Records of the Second Presbyterian Church of Brooklyn. Baptisms, 1832-1854; marriages, 1831-1859; history and lists of members,
1833-1861. (Typed.) [396
NBLiHi.

———— Vital records of Bushwick, Flatlands and Flatbush for 1847,
1848 and 1851, copied from the County Clerk's records. (Typed.) [397
NBLiHi.

———— Old Cutchogue cemetery inscriptions. (Typed.) [398
NBLiHi.

———— Cemetery on the side road leading from the main road at the
schoolhouse, East Marion. 1940. (Typed.) [399
NBLiHi.

———— Greenport cemeteries. 1940. (Typed.) [400
Inscriptions in the Sterling cemetery and in the cemetery at Webb Ave. and Third St.
NBLiHi.

———— Marriages and deaths from newspapers published on Long Island, 1791-1898. 2 vols. (Typed.)   [401
NBLiHi.

———— New Utrecht. Later inscriptions from the burying ground of the Protestant Reformed Dutch Church of New Utrecht (supplementing the transcript made by Teunis G. Bergen).   [402
NBLiHi.

———— Inscriptions from the cemetery at Northville. (Typed.)   [403
NBLiHi.

———— Some of the older stones from St. Patrick's Roman Catholic cemetery at Southold. 1941. (Typed.)   [404
NBLiHi.

Huntington, Edna and Alberta Pantle. Inscriptions from cemeteries in Orient Point (Terry-Tuthill and Latham-Beebe).   [405
NBLiHi.

Huntington, Edna; Harriet and Kenn Stryker-Rodda. Vital records from the *Long Island Farmer* and *Queens County Advertiser*. 1821-1841. 3 vols. (Typed.)   [406
NBLiHi.

Huntington, New York. Records, First Church, Huntington, New York; pastorates of the Rev. John Close and others, beginning in 1761. (Typed.)   [407
NBLiHi, NHuHi.

———— Index of early town meetings, trustees' proceedings, court records and surveys of Huntington, Long Island. (Typed.)   [408
NNNGB.

Huntting, J(ames) Madison. Marriages and deaths from the diary of J. Madison Huntting, 1841-1868. 2 vols. (Original and typed copy.) [409
NBLiHi.

Huntting, J. W. Copy of the records (1694-1853) of the First Church of Christ in Southold, July, 1858. (MS.)   [410
NBLiHi.

Huntting, Rev. Nathaniel. Records of the First Church of East Hampton, New York. In *New York Geneal. and Biog. Record, 24*, p. 183; *25*, pp. 35, 139, 196; *26*, p. 38; *28*, p. 109; *29*, pp. 18, 166; *30*, p. 40; *33*, pp. 81, 150, 223; and *34*, pp. 7, 112, 166, 251.   [411
Az, C, CaOTP, CL, CoD, CSf, Ct, CtHi, CtY, DLC, DNDAR, IaHi, IC, ICN, ICU, In, MB, MBAt, MBNEH, MdBP, MeHi, MH, MHi, Mi, MiD-B, MNF, MnHi, MnM, MoK, MoS, MWA, N, NB, NBLiHi, NBu, NBuG, Nc, NEh, Nh, NHC, NHi, NIC, NjNbS, NjPla, NJQ, NN, NNC, NNNGB, NR, OC, OCHP, OCl, OClWHi, OHi, PEa, PEr, PHi, PPi, PPL, USlGS, Wa, WaS, WM.

Huntting, Teunis D(imon). Associators of the town of East Hampton, April, 1775. (MS.)   [412
NBLiHi.

———— Long Island Genealogies. (MS.) [413
NBLiHi.

Hutchinson, Benjamin, Town Clerk. Records, town of Brookhaven, up to 1800; as compiled by the Town Clerk. 1880. [414
DLC, MBNEH, MWA, N, NBLiHi, NHu, NJQ (has an index), NN, NNC, NNNGB, NRvS, NSmB.

Hyde, E. Belcher. Atlas of the Brooklyn borough of the city of New York, originally Kings County. 1898-1899. 3 vols. [415
NB, NJQ (vols. 1, 3), NN.

Innes, John H. The earliest records of Brookhaven (Setauket). In *New York History, 16,* No. 4, pp. 436, 448. [416
CSmH, CSt, CU, CoT, Ct, CtHi, CtY, DLC, ICN, ICU, IEN, In, InU, IU, KHi, MH, MHi, MNS, MWA, MWiW, MdBJ, MiD-B, MnHi, N, NB, NBLiHi, NBn, NBP, NBu, NCH, NHi, NIC, NJQ, NN, NNA, NNC, NNU, NRU, NSU, NStC, NcU, NdU, NjP, OCl, OHi, PU, Vt, VW, WHi, WaU.

———— Extracts from the records of Newtown. Newspaper clippings. 2 vols. [416a
NBLiHi.

———— Ancient Newtown, formerly Middleburg, and other [!] newspaper clippings relating to Newtown. Marginal notes by the author. NJQ. [417

Ireland, Gordon. Huntington, Long Island, cemetery inscriptions. (A private cemetery in South Huntington.) In *New York Geneal. and Biog. Record, 60,* p. 264. [418
Az, C, CaOTP, CL, CoD, CSf, Ct. CtHi, CtY, DLC, DNDAR, IaHi, IC, ICN, ICU, In, MB, MBAt, MBNEH, MdBP, MeHi, MH, MHi, Mi, MiD-B, MNF, MnHi, MnM, MoK, MoS, MWA, N, NB, NBLiHi, NBu, NBuG, Nc, NEh, Nh, NHC, NHi, NIC, NjNbS, NjPla, NJQ, NN, NNC, NNNGB, NR, OC, OCHP, OCl, OClWHi, OHi, PEa, PEr, PHi, PPi, PPL, USlGS, Wa, WaS, WM.

Islip, New York. List of tax-payers, 1757. (MS.) [419
NBLiHi.

Jamaica, New York. Original assessment roll for the town of Jamaica . . . for 1834, alphabetically arranged. (MS.) [420
NNNGB.

———— Ditmas-Bennett burying ground at Jamaica. Mounted clippings from the *Brooklyn Daily Eagle.* September 5, 1915. [421
NBLiHi.

———— Jamaica local papers, 1743-1872. 1 folder. [422
NHi.

———— Papers concerning Jamaica, 1655-1685. (MS.) [423
NN (Manuscript Room).

———— Jamaica, Long Island, New York, Town Records, 1749-1897. Vols. 4, 5, 6. (Typed.) [424
NJQ, NNNGB (microfilm).

———— Abstracts of wills on file in the office of the County Clerk at

Jamaica.   Libers A, B, C.   [425
NNNGB (microfilm).

———————— Records of the village of Jamaica, 1814-1875.   1940.   (Typed.)
NJQ.   [426

Jarvis. Joel.   Book of marriages solemnized by me, made January 13,
1828.   (Typed.) 1937.   [427
Mr. Jarvis was Justice of the Peace at Huntington, New York.
NJQ.

Jefferson, Wayland.   Cutchogue, Southold's first colony.   1940.   [428
Includes the church records of Cutchogue, pp. 142-166.
DLC, DNDAR, MBNEH, NBLiHi, NEh, NJQ, NN, NNNGB.

———————— Southold and its people in the Revolutionary days.   1932.   [429
ICN, MB, MWA, N, NBLiHi, NEh, NJQ, NN, NNNGB, NSmB.

———————— Records of the First Church of Southold, Long Island.   In *New
York Geneal. and Biog. Record, 64,* pp. 217, 322; *65,* pp. 47, 152, 261,
329; *66,* pp. 51, 257, 293.   [430
Az, C, CaOTP, CL, CoD, CSf, Ct, CtHi, CtY, DLC, DNDAR, IaHi, IC, ICN, ICU,
In, MB, MBAt, MBNEH, MdBP, MeHi, MH, MHi, Mi, MiD-B, MNF, MnHi,
MnM, MoK, MoS, MWA, N, NB, NBLiHi, NBu, NBuG, Nc, NEh, Nh, NHC, NHi,
NIC, NjNbS, NjPla, NJQ, NN, NNC, NNNGB, NR, OC, OCHP, OCl, OClWHi,
OHi, PEa, PEr, PHi, PPi, PPL, USlGS, Wa, WaS, WM.

Johnson, ---, "Dr."   Records: births, marriages and deaths, St. George's
Church, Flushing, New York.   [431
NN (microfilm).

Johnston, Guy E.   Detailed history of the original township of Huntington, 1653-1860.   1926.   [432
NBLiHi, NJQ.

Jones, John H.   Inscriptions of gravestones, Huntington, Long Island.   In
New York Geneal. and Biog. Record, 31, pp. 113, 147, 247; *32,* pp. 47, 93,
176, 278; *33,* p. 97; *60,* p. 264.   [433
Az, C, CaOTP, CL, CoD, CSf, Ct, CtHi, CtY, DLC, DNDAR, IaHi, IC, ICN, ICU,
In, MB, MBAt, MBNEH, MdBP, MeHi, MH, MHi, Mi, MiD-B, MNF, MnHi,
MnM, MoK, MoS, MWA, N, NB, NBLiHi, NBu, NBuG, Nc, NEh, Nh, NHC, NHi,
NIC, NjNbS, NjPla, NJQ, NN, NNC, NNNGB, NR, OC, OCHP, OCl, OClWHi,
OHi, PEa, PEr, PHi, PPi, PPL, USlGS, Wa, WaS, WM.

———————— Oyster Bay, New York.   Inscriptions on Gravestones in the
Youngs Family Burial Grounds at Oyster Bay Cove.   In *New York
Geneal. and Biog. Record, 31,* p. 111.   [434
Az, C, CaOTP, CL, CoD, CSf, Ct, CtHi, CtY, DLC, DNDAR, IaHi, IC, ICN, ICU,
In, MB, MBAt, MBNEH, MdBP, MeHi, MH, MHi, Mi, MiD-B, MNF, MnHi,
MnM, MoK, MoS, MWA, N, NB, NBLiHi, NBu, NBuG, Nc, NEh, Nh, NHC, NHi,
NIC, NjNbS, NjPla, NJQ, NN, NNC, NNNGB, NR, OC, OCHP, OCl, OClWHi,
OHi, PEa, PEr, PHi, PPi, PPL, USlGS, Wa, WaS, WM.

Kelby, Robert H.   New York Marriage Licenses in the archives of the
New York Historical Society.   1916.   [435
DLC, DNDAR, MBNEH, NBLiHi, NNNGB.

———————— New York Marriage Licenses, originals in the archives of the

New York Historical Society. In *New York Geneal. and Biog. Record*, *46*, pp. 279, 337; *47*, pp. 68, 176, 286.   [436

Az, C, CaOTP, CL, CoD, CSf, Ct, CtHi, CtY, DLC, DNDAR, IaHi, IC, ICN, ICU, In, MB, MBAt, MBNEH, MdBP, MeHi, MH, MHi, Mi, MiD-B, MNF, MnHi, MnM, MoK, MoS, MWA, N, NB, NBLiHi, NBu, NBuG, Nc, NEh, Nh, NHC, NHi, NIC, NjNbS, NjPla, NJQ, NN, NNC, NNNGB, NR, OC, OCHP, OCl, OClWHi, OHi, PEa, PEr, PHi, PPi, PPL, USlGS, Wa, WaS, WM.

Kelby, William. Brookhaven (Long Island) Epitaphs. In *New York Geneal. and Biog. Record, 10*, p. 48; *16*, p. 131; *17*, p. 259; and *21*, p. 73.
                                                                             [437

Az, C, CaOTP, CL, CoD, CSf, Ct, CtHi, CtY, DLC, DNDAR, IaHi, IC, ICN, ICU, In, MB, MBAt, MBNEH, MdBP, MeHi, MH, MHi, Mi, MiD-B, MNF, MnHi, MnM, MoK, MoS, MWA, N, NB, NBLiHi, NBu, NBuG, Nc, NEh, Nh, NHC, NHi, NIC, NjNbS, NjPla, NJQ, NN, NNC, NNNGB, NR, OC, OCHP, OCl, OClWHi, OHi, PEa, PEr, PHi, PPi, PPL, USlGS, Wa, WaS, WM.

———— Floyd Epitaphs at Setauket, Long Island. In *New York Geneal. and Biog. Record, 15*, p. 41.   [438

Az, C, CaOTP, CL, CoD, CSf, Ct, CtHi, CtY, DLC, DNDAR, IaHi, IC, ICN, ICU, In, MB, MBAt, MBNEH, MdBP, MeHi, MH, MHi, Mi, MiD-B, MNF, MnHi, MnM, MoK, MoS, MWA, N, NB, NBLiHi, NBu, NBuG, Nc, NEh, Nh, NHC, NHi, NIC, NjNbS, NjPla, NJQ, NN, NNC, NNNGB, NR, OC, OCHP, OCl, OClWHi, OHi, PEa, PEr, PHi, PPi, PPL, USlGS, Wa, WaS, WM.

Kelsey, J. S. History of Long Island City, New York. 1896.   [439

DLC, MWA, NBLiHi, NJQ, NN.

Kent, Charles N. An historical sketch of Merrick, Long Island, 1643-1900. 1900.   [440

DLC, MWA, N, NBLiHi, NJQ, NN, NNC, NSmB.

King, Mrs. Edna B. Records of the Bennett cemetery (East Hampton, New York). Copied 1941.   [441

NEh.

———— Records of the Nominick Hills (East Hampton) cemetery. Copied 1941.   [442

NEh.

———— Records of the Ranger cemetery (East Hampton). Copied 1941.
                                                                             [443
NEh.

———— Records of the Russell-Payne cemetery (East Hampton). Copied 1941.   [444

NEh.

———— Records of the Terry cemetery (East Hampton). Copied 1941.
                                                                             [445
NEh.

King, Mrs. L. Leroy. Cemetery records of the Presbyterian Churchyard in Setauket, Long Island, up to January 1, 1883. (Typed.)   [446

NEh.

———— Cemetery and church records of private graveyards in Setauket and in Northwest. (Typed.)   [447

NEh.

King, Rufus. Genealogical items from the *Long Island Star*. In *New York Geneal. and Biog. Record, 48*, p. 411.   [448

Az, C, CaOTP, CL, CoD, CSf, Ct, CtHi, CtY, DLC, DNDAR, IaHi, IC, ICN, ICU, In, MB, MBAt, MBNEH, MdBP, MeHi, MH, MHi, Mi, MiD-B, MNF, MnHi, MnM, MoK, MoS, MWA, N, NB, NBLiHi, NBu, NBuG, Nc, NEh, Nh, NHC, NHi, NIC, NjNbS, NjPla, NJQ, NN, NNC, NNNGB, NR, OC, OCHP, OCl, OClWHi, OHi, PEa, PEr, PHi, PPi, PPL, USlGS, Wa, WaS, WM.

———— Long Island marriages and deaths from the *Suffolk Gazette*. In *New York Geneal. and Biog. Record, 24*, pp. 86, 159; *25*, pp. 6, 89, 137, 161.   [449

Az, C, CaOTP, CL, CoD, CSf, Ct, CtHi, CtY, DLC, DNDAR, IaHi, IC, ICN, ICU, In, MB, MBAt, MBNEH, MdBP, MeHi, MH, MHi, Mi, MiD-B, MNF, MnHi, MnM, MoK, MoS, MWA, N, NB, NBLiHi, NBu, NBuG, Nc, NEh, Nh, NHC, NHi, NIC, NjNbS, NjPla, NJQ, NN, NNC, NNNGB, NR, OC, OCHP, OCl, OClWHi, OHi, PEa, PEr, PHi, PPi, PPL, USlGS, Wa, WaS, WM.

———— Inscriptions from the cemetery in Orient, Long Island. The Oyster Ponds Cemetery. In *New York Geneal. and Biog. Record, 6*, pp. 107-109.   [450

Az, C, CaOTP, CL, CoD, CSf, Ct, CtHi, CtY, DLC, DNDAR, IaHi, IC, ICN, ICU, In, MB, MBAt, MBNEH, MdBP, MeHi, MH, MHi, Mi, MiD-B, MNF, MnHi, MnM, MoK, MoS, MWA, N, NB, NBLiHi, NBu, NBuG, Nc, NEh, Nh, NHC, NHi, NIC, NjNbS, NjPla, NJQ, NN, NNC, NNNGB, NR, OC, OCHP, OCl, OClWHi, OHi, PEa, PEr, PHi, PPi, PPL, USlGS, Wa, WaS, WM.

Kings County, New York. Kings County assessment rolls, 1838-1841, 1843, 1845 and 1853-1854. (Originals.)   [451
NN (Manuscript Room).

———— Inscriptions from the Schenck burying ground, Kings County. NBLiHi.   [452

———— Marriages in Kings County, 1864-1865, from the state census of 1865. (Typed.)   [453
NBLiHi.

———— Miscellaneous papers of Kings County, 1669-1800. Includes marriages, New Utrecht, New York; Van Brunt land papers, etc. [454
NN (Manuscript Room).

———— Abstracts of wills, County of Kings, 1787-1822.   [455
NJQ.

Kings County Genealogical Club Collections. Baptisms in the Reformed Dutch Church of Brooklyn, as translated by the late Hon. T. G. Bergen. Vol. I, No. 4, p. 56, with continuations.   [456
This was reprinted from the Brooklyn Corporation Manual for 1869.
DLC, DNDAR, MBNEH, NBLiHi, NEh, NJQ, NN, NNNGB, USlGS.

———— Reformed Dutch Church cemetery (inscriptions), Flatlands, 1882-1894. Vol. I, No. 2, p. 17.   [457
DLC, DNDAR, MBNEH, NBLiHi, NEh, NJQ, NN, NNNGB, USlGS.

———— Reformed Dutch Church cemetery (inscriptions), Gravesend. 1882-1894. Vol. I, No. 3, p. 31.   [458
DLC, DNDAR, MBNEH, NBLiHi, NEh, NJQ, NN, NNNGB, USlGS.

———— Reformed Dutch Church cemetery (inscriptions), New Utrecht,

1882-1894. Vol. I, No. 1, p. 1.   [459
DLC, DNDAR, MBNEH, NBLiHi, NEh, NJQ, NN, NNNGB, USIGS.

Knowles, C. J. Church records of the Rev. C. J. Knowles of Bellport,
Riverhead and Fireplace, Long Island. Copied by Lucy D. Akerly.
1900. (MS.)   [460
NNNGB.

———— Book kept by C. J. Knowles of the Congregational Church, Riverhead (New York). Marriages, 1833-1850; baptisms, 1836-1850; and
deaths, 1834-1850. Also, a list of church members and accounts. Copied
by Orville B. Ackerly in Ackerly Deed Book No. 10, pp. 70-80. (See
No. 7.)   [461
NEh.

Ladd, Horatio Oliver. The origin and history of Grace Church (Protestant Episcopal), Jamaica, New York. 1914.   [462
Contains records kept by the Rev. Thomas Poyer and others: Baptisms from 1710;
marriages, 1710-1731, 1769—; funerals 1710-1731.
DLC, DNDAR, MBNEH, MWA, NBLiHi, NEh, NJQ, NN, NNNGB, USIGS.

Lain and Healy's Directories. Brooklyn and Long Island Business Direc-
tory. (See also No. 74.)   [463
DLC, 1875/78, 1883/96; MWA, 1874, 1892; NB, 1877/78-1878/79, 1881/82-1897;
NBLiHi, 1875/76, 1877/78, 1880/81-1881/82, 1883/84-1890/91, 1892, 1895, 1898;
NN, 1874, 1877/78-1878/79, 1882/83, 1884/85, 1886/87, 1888/89, 1890/91, 1892;
NJQ, 1881/82-1883/84, 1888/89, 1891/92, 1894-97.

Lake Grove, New York. Quarterly conferences, Lake Grove Methodist
Episcopal Church, 1795-1817, 1853-1854, 1873-1902. (MS.)   [464
NN (Manuscript Room).

Landon Family. Landon family papers (17th to 19th centuries). (MS.)
NBLiHi, NEh (letters, 1792-1830; deeds).   [465

Lant, J. H. Hempstead and Freeport directory, containing a general directory of the inhabitants and a classified business directory.   [466
MWA, 1897, 1901/02, 1905/06, 1909/10, 1911/12; NJQ, 1913/14, 1915/16; NN, 1897,
1901/02, 1903/04, 1905/06, 1907/08, 1915/16.

Lawson, Harriet Dondero. Olde Flushing. 1952.   [467
DLC, NBLiHi, NEh, NJQ, NN, NNNGB.

Ledley, Wilson Van D. Index to the first book of records of the Dutch
Reformed Church of Brooklyn (New York), 1660-1719. 1957.   [468
This indexes the edition published by the Holland Society, but the index is usable
with other transcripts, as references are by months and years.
NBLiHi, NNHol.

Lewis Publishing Company. Montauk business directory; the Long Island
Red Book; Queens, Nassau and Suffolk counties. 1913-15, titled The
Montauk business directory of Long Island: Queens, Nassau and Suffolk
Counties.   [469
DLC, 1913; NB, 1913-1914; NJQ, 1913; NN, 1913, 1915-1917.

Long Island, New York. Documents relating to conveyances of land, etc. on Long Island, 1660-1702/3.   [470
DLC, N, NBLiHi, NEh, NJQ.

———— Sketches of Long Island, from the *Brooklyn Standard*, 1864-1867. Mounted clippings.   [471
NBLiHi.

Long Island City, New York. Long Island City directory. 1901(?), 1906.
NJQ.   [472

Long Island Democrat (newspaper). Card name index (45 drawers) of births, marriages and deaths in the *Long Island Democrat*, the *Newtown Register*, the *Corrector* (Sag Harbor, New York) and other newspapers of Long Island.   [473
NJQ.

Long Island Historical Society. Brooklyn and Long Island scrapbooks. (Historical and genealogical.) 146 vols. with analytical card index.
NBLiHi.   [474

Long Island Traveler (newspaper). Births, marriages and deaths from the *Long Island Traveler*. Mounted clippings.   [475
NBLiHi, NEh (incomplete).

———— Long Island genealogy; questions and answers. Mounted clippings from the *Long Island Traveler*, 1897-1916.   [476
Not all libraries listed have a complete file.
NBLiHi, NEh, NN, NNNGB, NRvS.

Long Island Wills. Miscellaneous wills of Long Islanders, 1700 to 1920. Transcripts of 396 wills with index.   [477
NEh.

MacCormack, Elizabeth J(anet). Abstracts of wills, 1848-1856, Queens County. (Typed.)   [478
NNNGB.

———— Burials in Springfield cemetery. (Typed.)   [479
NNNGB.

———— Inscriptions from six cemeteries of Suffolk County, New York. (Typed.)   [480
BROOKHAVEN: Woodhull family yard near Mastic Beach.
SOUTH HAVEN: Presbyterian Church cemetery.
YAPHANK: St. Andrews Episcopalian, Baptist, and Presbyterian Church cemeteries; Hawkins family burying ground.
NBLiHi, NN.

MacDonald, James M(adison). Two centuries in the history of the Presbyterian Church in Jamaica, New York. 1862. Contains the rate lists for 1683 and 1708/9.   [481
CU, DLC, DNDAR, MBNEH, MWA, N, NBLiHi, NEh, NHu, NjP, NJQ, NN, NNC, NSmB, PHi, PPPrHi.

Mallman, Rev. Jacob. Historical papers on Shelter Island and its Presbyterian Church, with genealogical tables. 1899. [482
DLC, DNDAR, MB, MBNEH, MWA, N, NBLiHi, NEh, NHi, NHu, NHuHi, NjP, NJQ, NN, NNNGB, NSmB, USlGS.

Mandeville, G(iles) Henry. Flushing, Past and Present. 1860. [483
CSmH, MWA, N, NB, NBLiHi, NEh, NJQ, NN, NNNGB, NSmB, PHi, PPL.

Massapequa, New York. Tombstone inscriptions in the old burial ground on the south side of the South County Road a few hundred feet west of Ocean avenue, Massapequa, Long Island. [484
NEh.

Mather, Frederic G(regory). The Refugees of 1776 from Long Island to Connecticut. 1913. [485
DLC, DNDAR, ICHi, MB, MBNEH, MiU, MWA, N, NB, NBLiHi, NEh, NHu, NHuHi, NIC, NjNbS, NjP, NJQ, NN, NNNGB, NRvS, NSmB, OCl, OClWHi, OU, USlGS.

Mattituck, New York, Chamber of Commerce. Mattituck and Its Vicinity: A directory. 1933. [486
NJQ.

McDougall, Rev. James. Marriages, Huntington Presbyterian Church, 1836-1853. Transcribed by Orville B. Ackerly, recorded in Ackerly Deed Book No. 10, pp. 81-91. (Part of No. 7.) [487
NEh.

McQueen, David. Abstracts of Deeds, Kings County, New York. In *New York Geneal. and Biog. Record, 48,* pp. 110, 291, 355. [488
Az, C, CaOTP, CL, CoD, CSf, Ct, CtHi, CtY, DLC, DNDAR, IaHi, IC, ICN, ICU, In, MB, MBAt, MBNEH, MdBP, MeHi, MH, MHi, Mi, MiD-B, MNF, MnHi, MnM, MoK, MoS, MWA, N, NB, NBLiHi, NBu, NBuG, Nc, NEh, Nh, NHC, NHi, NIC, NjNbS, NjPla, NJQ, NN, NNC, NNNGB, NR, OC, OCHP, OCl, OClWHi, OHi, PEa, PEr, PHi, PPi, PPL, USlGS, Wa, WaS, WM.

————— Abstracts of Wills, Kings County. In *New York Geneal. and Biog. Record, 47,* pp. 161, 227. [489
Az, C, CaOTP, CL, CoD, CSf, Ct, CtHi, CtY, DLC, DNDAR, IaHi, IC, ICN, ICU, In, MB, MBAt, MBNEH, MdBP, MeHi, MH, MHi, Mi, MiD-B, MNF, MnHi, MnM, MoK, MoS, MWA, N, NB, NBLiHi, NBu, NBuG, Nc, NEh, Nh, NHC, NHi, NIC, NjNbS, NjPla, NJQ, NN, NNC, NNNGB, NR, OC, OCHP, OCl, OClWHi, OHi, PEa, PEr, PHi, PPi, PPL, USlGS, Wa, WaS, WM.

————— Index to Queens County Wills, 1687-1762, with (inscriptions from the) town burial ground, Newtown; Fort Hill cemetery, Oyster Bay; and the Weekes cemetery, Spring Hill (Muttontown). 1899. (MS.) [490
NBLiHi.

Meier, Evelyn R(owley). The Wading River—Pauguaconsuk. 1955. [491
NBLiHi, NJQ, NN.

Meigs, Alice H. Cemetery inscriptions in the Buffet burying ground,

Dix Hills.   1936.   [492
NJQ.

————— Nassau County cemeteries (inscriptions).   1 vol.   [493
AMITYVILLE: Old cemetery (County Line road), supplemental pages.
CENTRAL PARK: Stymus cemetery, pp. 55-57.
EAST NORWICH: Locust cemetery (route 106 between Brookville Road and
    Muttontown road), pp. 100-104; Wesley Methodist Episcopal Church cemetery,
    pp. 58-71.
JERUSALEM: Jackson cemetery, pp. 96-99.
MASSAPEQUA: Fort Neck cemetery, supplemental pages.
NORTH BETHPAGE: Powell cemetery, pp. 104c-104e.
PLAINEDGE: Combs cemetery (on Seamans Neck road north of Southern State
    Parkway), pp. 91-92; Powell cemetery, p. 104a.
PLAINVIEW: Van Wyck cemetery, p. 104b.
PORT WASHINGTON: Free Church cemetery, pp. 72-79; Mitchell cemetery, pp.
    89-90.
ROSLYN: Roslyn cemetery, pp. 2-54a.
SEA CLIFF: Carpenter cemetery, pp. 85-88.
SEARINGTOWN: Methodist churchyard, pp. 93-95.
WOODBURY: Methodist Episcopal churchyard, pp. 80-82; Valentine cemetery, pp.
    83-84.
NJQ.

————— Suffolk county cemeteries (Inscriptions).   7 vols. 193—.   [494
AMAGANSETT: Miller cemetery (near Abram's Landing), I, pp. 167-168; Parsons
    cemetery, I, pp. 134-135.
ARSHAMOMAQUE: Cemetery, I, pp. 242-248.
BABYLON: Rural cemetery, I, pp. 1-100; Van Cott tombstone, IV, p. 40.
BELLPORT: Old village cemetery (Academy lane), V, p. 72.
BROOKHAVEN: Conklin cemetery, I, p. 132; Hawkins cemetery, III, pp. 59-60;
    Hulse cemetery, I, pp. 207-208; Miller cemetery, I, pp. 209-210; Robinson ceme-
    tery, IV, p. 31; Rose cemetery, III, pp. 56-57; Village cemetery, VII, pp. 26-33.
CANOE PLACE: Paul Cuffee grave, I, p. 130.
CENTEREACH: Hallock cemetery, IV, p. 19; Hammond cemetery, IV, p. 22.
CENTRE MORICHES: Bishop cemetery, VII, p. 3; Cemetery, VII, pp. 1-2; Havens-
    Young cemetery, V, pp. 94-95.
COMMACK: Brown cemetery, III, p. 50; Burr cemetery (on Burr ave.), VII, p.
    53; Burr cemetery (on Jericho turnpike), III, pp. 46-47; Commack cemetery,
    III, pp. 61-101; Smith cemetery, III, pp. 48-49; Wicks cemetery, III, pp. 52-53.
CORAM: Baptist churchyard, I, pp. 221-227; Bayles cemetery, IV, pp. 20-21; Haw-
    kins cemetery, I, pp. 154-156; Mott-Fordham cemetery, I, pp. 152-153; Still
    cemetery, I, p. 150.
CUTCHOGUE: Cutchogue cemetery, I, pp. 171-206.
DIX HILLS: Buffett cemetery, III, pp. 41-45; Carll cemetery, III, pp. 37-38; Old
    cemetery, III, pp. 39-40.
EAST HAMPTON: Bennett cemetery, VII, p. 14; Edwards cemetery, I, pp. 228-229;
    King cemetery, VII, p. 13; Town cemetery, V, pp. 33-38.
EAST MARION: Tuthill cemetery, I, pp. 240-241.
ELWOOD: Old cemetery (north of Elwood on east side of Elwood road), IV, p. 26.
FIRE PLACE LANDING: Parsons cemetery, I, pp. 141-144.
FLANDERS: Fanning cemetery, III, p. 58.
FREETOWN: Parsons cemetery, I, pp. 136-140.
GREENLAWN: Oakes cemetery (north of Jericho turnpike, near Greenlawn), IV,
    p. 29.
HALF HOLLOW HILLS: Carman cemetery (Half Hollows Road, near Carman
    road), IV, p. 38; Conklin cemetery, IV, pp. 47-49; Nostrand cemetery (on Half
    Hollows road), IV, p. 39.
HAMPTON BAYS: Squires cemetery, I, pp. 162-163.
HAUPPAUGE: Blydenburgh cemetery, IV, pp. 99-100; Methodist Episcopal church-
    yard, IV, pp. 68-96; Wheeler cemetery, IV, pp. 97-98.
HITHER PLAINS (MONTAUK): Hand cemetery, I, pp. 148-149.

HUNTINGTON: Gardiner cemetery, V, p. 49; Gildersleeve cemetery, VII, p. 51; Hawkins-Mulford cemetery (between Huntington and Kings Park), I, pp. 145-147.

HUNTINGTON SOUTH: Oldfields cemetery, IV, pp. 44-46.

LAKE RONKONKOMA: Methodist churchyard, V, pp. 17-32b.

MANORVILLE: Brookfield Presbyterian churchyard, V. pp. 77-80a; Methodist Protestant churchyard, V, pp. 73-76; Raynor cemetery, IV, p. 18.

MASTIC NECK: Woodhull cemetery, IV, pp. 64-65.

MELVILLE: Ketcham cemetery, pp. 15-16; Melville cemetery (formerly Presbyterian cemetery), III, pp. 1-14; Methodist cemetery, III, pp. 17-27.

MIDDLE ISLAND: Methodist Episcopal churchyard, I, pp. 167-170; Union cemetery, IV, pp. 101-125.

MILLERS PLACE: Davis cemetery (between Mt. Sinai and Millers Place), IV, p. 52.

MORICHES: Baldwin grave, I, p. 133; Hawkins cemetery (Pine Neck), VII, pp. 4-5.

MOUNT SINAI: Cemetery (back of church), IV, pp. 62-63; Davis cemetery, pp. 53-55; Davis cemetery (2 graves), IV, p. 58; Davis-Norton-Phillips cemetery, IV, pp. 59-61; Tuthill-Davis cemetery, IV, pp. 56-57.

NEW VILLAGE: First Congregational churchyard, V, pp. 52-71.

NORTH HAVEN: Hamilton cemetery, I, p. 131; Payne cemetery, I, pp. 165-166.

NORTHPORT: Scudder cemetery, I, pp. 157-159; VII, p. 52.

NORTH SEA: North Sea cemetery, I, pp. 211-220.

NORTHWEST HARBOR (EAST HAMPTON): Edwards cemetery, VII, p. 15; Ranger cemetery, VII, p. 16.

OAKDALE: St. John's Protestant Episcopal churchyard, V, pp. 96-101.

OLD FIELD: Cemetery near the lighthouse, IV, pp. 12-14.

ORIENT POINT: Beebe cemetery, I, pp. 230-235; Terry cemetery, I, pp. 236-239.

PATCHOGUE: Cedar Grove cemetery, IV, p. 23 (oldest stones only).

PORT JEFFERSON: Cedar Hill cemetery, VI, pp. 46-134.

RIDGE: Aldrich cemetery, IV, p. 66.

ROCKY POINT: Hallock cemetery, V, pp. 40-42.

SAG HARBOR: Oakland cemetery, II, pp. 1-213.

ST. JAMES: Field cemetery, IV, pp. 7-8; Methodist Episcopal churchyard, V, pp. 50-51a; Mills cemetery (at Mill Pond), IV, pp. 1-5; Smith cemetery (on Moriches road), IV, p. 6.

SAYVILLE: St. Ann's Protestant Episcopal cemetery, VII, pp. 54-80.

SELDEN: Longbothum cemetery, I, pp. 160-161.

SETAUKET: Biggs cemetery, V, p. 48; Thompson cemetery, IV, pp. 27-28.

SMITHTOWN: Bell cemetery, IV, p. 51.

SMITHTOWN BRANCH: Smithtown Presbyterian church cemetery, VI, pp. 1-44.

SMITHTOWN LANDING (VILLAGE OF THE LANDING): Methodist Episcopal churchyard, V, pp. 1-16a; Vail cemetery, IV, p. 50.

SOUTH HAVEN: Barteau cemetery, IV, pp. 41-43; Hawkins cemetery, IV, p. 67; Miller cemetery, V, pp. 44-45; Presbyterian churchyard, III, pp. 54-55.

SOUTH MANOR: Village cemetery, V, pp. 81-93.

SPRINGS, THE (EAST HAMPTON): Davis cemetery, VII, p. 8; Edwards cemetery, VII, p. 7; Edwards cemetery (another), VII, p. 9; Parsons cemetery, VII, p. 12; Springs Presbyterian chapel yard, VII, pp. 10-11.

STONY BROOK: Davis cemetery, IV, pp. 9-11; Hawkins cemetery, IV, pp. 32-35; Smith cemetery (back of Stony Brook hotel and west of Railroad avenue), IV, pp. 15-17.

SWEZEYTOWN: Swezey cemetery, V, pp. 46-47.

WADING RIVER: Cemetery (shore road), I, pp. 253-255.

WESTHAMPTON: Wells-Jagger cemetery, VII, pp. 23-24.

WEST HILLS: Chichester cemetery (Halsey road), V, p. 43; Methodist churchyard, III, pp. 28-36.

WEST ISLIP: Thompson cemetery (Sagtikos Manor), V, p. 39.

WYANDANCH: Old cemetery, VII, p. 25.

YAPHANK: Cemetery, I, p. 249; Baptist cemetery, VII, pp. 21-22; Cemetery association, VII, pp. 34-50; Hawkins cemetery, I, pp. 126-129; Presbyterian churchyard, I, pp. 250-252; St. Andrews Episcopal churchyard, VII, pp. 17-20.

Meigs, Alice H., and Charles U. Powell. Description of private and family cemeteries in the borough of Queens. 1932. (Issued through the Queens-borough Topographical Bureau.)   [494a
DLC, MBNEH, NBLiHi, NEh, NJQ, NN.

Melville, New York. Records of the Sweet Hollow Presbyterian Church at Melville (Huntington), New York. (Typed.)   [495
NHuHi.

Merle-Smith, Van Santvoord. The Village of Oyster Bay, its founding and growth from 1653 to 1700. 1953.   [496
Includes the names of freeholders, 1653-1702.
DLC, NBLiHi, NEh, NJQ, NN, NNNGB.

Metropolitan Directory Co. Morris' directory of Jamaica, N. Y., 1921/22, including Hollis and Queens Village.   [497
DLC, NJQ.

————— The 1922/23 directory of Richmond Hill and Woodhaven, New York, including Kew Gardens, Forest Hills and Ozone Park.   [498
DLC, NJQ, NN.

Metzger, Ethel and Marjorie Leek. Transcript of various cemeteries of Suffolk County. WPA microfilm.   [499
NJQ, NNNGB.

Middagh Family. Middagh family papers, 1709-1843. (Brooklyn, New York.)   [500
These include wills of this family and landpapers relating to the Brooklyn ferry.
NN (Manuscript Room).

Middle Island, New York. Middle Island Union cemetery records. 1947.   [501
NEh.

Miller, M. D. B. Some Inscriptions taken from the "Old Jackson Family" graveyard at Jerusalem, Long Island. In *New York Geneal. and Biog. Record, 26,* p. 79.   [502
Az, C, CaOTP, CL, CoD, CSf, Ct, CtHi, CtY, DLC, DNDAR, IaHi, IC, ICN, ICU, In, MB, MBAt, MBNEH, MdBP, MeHi, MH, MHi, MI, MiD-B, MNF, MnHi, MnM, MoK, MoS, MWA, N, NB, NBLiHi, NBu, NBuG, Nc, NEh, Nh, NHC, NHi, NIC, NjNbS, NjPla, NJQ, NN, NNC, NNNGB, NR, OC, OCHP, OCl, OClWHi, OHi, PEa, PEr, PHi, PPi, PPL, USlGS, Wa, WaS, WM.

————— Inscriptions from the Old Jones graveyard at West Neck, Huntington. In *New York Geneal. and Biog. Record, 26,* p. 45.   [503
Az, C, CaOTP, CL, CoD, CSf, Ct, CtHi, CtY, DLC, DNDAR, IaHi, IC, ICN, ICU, In, MB, MBAt, MBNEH, MdBP, MeHi, MH, MHi, Mi, MiD-B, MNF, MnHi, MnM, MoK, MoS, MWA, N, NB, NBLiHi, NBu, NBuG, Nc, NEh, Nh, NHC, NHi, NIC, NjNbS, NjPla, NJQ, NN, NNC, NNNGB, NR, OC, OCHP, OCl, OClWHi, OHi, PEa, PEr, PHi, PPi, PPL, USlGS, Wa, WaS, WM.

Miller, Robert M. Salmon records—giving marriages in Southold, L. I., and elsewhere from 1683 to 1811, copied from the original in the possession of Nathaniel Hubbard Cleveland. Deaths from 1684 to 1811. 1912-1913.   [504
NBLiHi.

Mitchell, William A. Huntington and Hempstead marriages. 1772-1826 and 1726-1779. (Typed.)   [505
NBLiHi.

Montauk, New York. Indian deeds. Montauk, 1655-1794. typed from the originals in the possession of the Long Island Historical Society. [506
NBLiHi.

Moore, Charles Benjamin. Early history of Hempstead. 1879. With a list of proprietors, 1647. Reprinted from the *New York Genealogical and Biographical Record.*   [507
DLC, N, NBLiHi, NJQ, NN, NRvS.

———— Historical address . . . Southold, L. I. 1890.   [508
NBLiHi, NJQ, NN, NNNGB.

———— Town of Southold, Long Island: Personal Index prior to 1698, and index of 1698. 1868.   [509
DLC, MBNEH, MWA, N, NBLiHi, NEh, NJQ, NN, NNNGB, NSmB, PPL, USlGS.

———— Inventories, Suffolk county, 1670-1692. In *New York Geneal. and Biog. Record, 12,* p. 132.   [510
Az, C, CaOTP, CL, CoD, CSf, Ct, CtHi, CtY, DLC, DNDAR, IaHi, IC, ICN, ICU, In, MB, MBAt, MBNEH, MdBP, MeHi, MH, MHi, Mi, MiD-B, MNF, MnHi, MnM, MoK, MoS, MWA, N, NB, NBLiHi, NBu, NBuG, Nc, NEh, Nh, NHC, NHi, NIC, NjNbS, NjPla, NJQ, NN, NNC, NNNGB, NR, OC, OCHP, OCl, OClWHi, OHi, PEa, PEr, PHi, PPi, PPL, USlGS, Wa, WaS, WM.

Moore, Rev. William H. History of St. George's Church, Hempstead (1704-1880). 1881.   [511
NBLiHi, NNNGB.

Morrell, John. Flatlands census, 1810. (Typed.)   [512
NBLiHi.

Mount Sinai, New York. Old Mans (Mount Sinai) vital records, 1795-1872.   [513
NEh.

Mulford, A. Cornell. Gravestone inscriptions from Oyster Bay and vicinity. 1935-1954.   [514
NEh.

Munsell and Co. History of Queens County, New York: with illustrations, portraits and sketches of prominent families and individuals. 1882. [515
DLC, MWA, N, NBLiHi, NHuHi, NIC, NJQ, NN, NNC, NNNGB, NSmB.

———— History of Suffolk County, New York, with illustrations, portraits and sketches of prominent families and individuals. 1882. [516
DLC, DNDAR, MBNEH, MWA, N, NBLiHi, NEh, NHu, NHuHi, NIC, NJQ, NN, NNNGB, NSmB, USlGS.

Murphy, Henry C(ruse). Memoranda taken from the tombstones in the old Dutch burying ground in Fulton avenue (street) near Smith street (Brooklyn, New York). 1863. (MS.)   [517
NBLiHi.

The same printed in *The Long Island Hist. Soc. Quarterly*, *1*, pp. 82-86.

CoD, Ct, CtY, CU, DLC, DSI-M, ICN, IU, MeU, MH, MHi, MiD-B, MnHi, MWA, N, NB, NBB, NBLiHi, NBP, NBuG, NEh, NjP, NJQ, NN, NNC, OHi, PCA, PHi, VW, WaU, WHi.

———— The Lefferts burying ground (inscriptions). *Circa* 1863. (MS.)
NBLiHi.   [518

The same, printed in *The Long Island Hist. Soc. Quarterly*, *4*, pp. 21-22.

CoD, Ct, CtY, CU, DLC, DSI-M, ICN, IU, MeU, MH, MHi, MiD-B, MnHi, MWA, N, NB, NBB, NBLiHi, NBP, NBuG, NEh, NjP, NJQ, NN, NNC, OHi, PCA, PHi, VW, WaU, WHi.

Nassau County, New York. Cemetery records, Nassau County. Plainview, Powell (Bethpage), Bethpage, Old Bethpage and Farmingdale cemeteries.   [519
NEh.

New Lots, New York. Records of the New Lots Reformed Church, 1824-1904 (?), vol. 1.   1938   [520
NJQ (typed); NN, NNNGB (microfilm).

New York City, New York: Common Council. Minutes of the Common Council of the City of New York, 1675-1776; 1784-1831.   29 vols.   [521
This series contains many references to settlers of Kings County, New York.
DLC, ICJ, ICN, IU, N, NBLiHi, NEh, NjP, NN, NNNGB, ViU, WaU.

New York County (and Province). New York wills. Abstracts of wills on file in the Surrogate's office, City of New York. Published in *Collections of the New York Historical Society*, vols. 25 to 41, inclusive.   [522
These contain many New York provincial wills.
DLC, DNDAR, DNGS, DN, MB, MBNEH, MdBP, MiU-C, NBLiHi, NEh, NjNbT, NjP, NJQ, NN, NNNGB, PMA, USIGS.

New York Genealogical and Biographical Society. Baptisms and marriages in the Reformed Dutch Church, New York, 1639-1800. *Collections of the New York Geneal. and Biog. Soc.*, vols. 1, 2, 3.   [523
DLC, NBLiHi, NHi, NN, NNNGB.

New York (Long Island). Bible Records. Many volumes, indexed. (Typed.)   [524
Collected by the various chapters of the Daughters of the American Revolution.
DNDAR.

———— Bible Records in alphabetical order by families. (Typed.) [525
MBNEH.

———— Bible Records (of Long Island families). Several volumes. (Typed.)   [526
NBLiHi.

New York: Secretary of the Province. Names of persons for whom marriage licenses were issued by the Secretary of the Province of New York previous to 1784. Issued by the Secretary of State. 1860. [527
DLC, NBLiHi, NJQ, NN, NNNGB.

New York State. Census records.   [528
Kings County, 1855, 1865, 1875, 1892, 1905, 1915, 1925.
KINGS COUNTY CLERK'S OFFICE; N (MSS. and History Section).

Nassau County, 1915, 1925.
NASSAU COUNTY CLERK'S OFFICE; N (MSS. and History Section).

Queens County, 1892, 1915, 1925.
QUEENS COUNTY CLERK'S OFFICE; N (MSS. and History Section).

Suffolk County, 1915, 1925.
N (MSS. and History Section).

New York State. Supplementary list of marriage licenses. In *Univ. State
Library Bulletin, History, No. 1,* April, 1898.   [529
DLC, DNDAR, NBLiHi, NJQ, NN, NNNGB.

Newtown, New York. Newtown (Elmhurst), New York. First Reformed
Church. Baptisms and marriages, 1736-1845; financial account, 1771-
1805 (written in Dutch through 1796) ; minutes of the Board of Elders,
1850-1910, and minutes of the consistory, 1731-1925. Several volumes.
(MS.)   [530
NJQ.

———— Military records, town of Newtown, Queens County. 1861-1886.
1939. (Typed.)   [531
NJQ.

———— Quit rent receipt book, 1706-1783. (MS.)   [532
This contains record of strays, 1794-1871, and the register of earmarks, 1813-1814.
NJQ.

———— Reformed Dutch Church. Baptisms and marriages, 1741-1845.
Kirk meisters book, 1731-1834.   [533
NN (microfilm).

———— Town records, 1656-1720. (Typed.)   [534
NBLiHi, NJQ.

———— Newtown tax lists, 1787; records of overseers of the poor, 1873-
1876. 2 vols.   [535
NHi.

North Brookhaven, New York. Historical sketches, settlements and vil-
lages of North Brookhaven town, 1655-1955.   [536
This title refers to the northern part of the town of Brookhaven. There is no such
town as North Brookhaven.
NJQ.

North Hempstead, New York. North Hempstead assessment roll, 1846.
(MS.)   [537
NBLiHi.

———— Christ Church, North Hempstead: subscription lists and cash
accounts, 1802-1834. (MS.)   [538
NBLiHi.

O'Brien, Michael J. Irish settlers in Queens County. In *Jour. of Amer. Irish Hist. Soc., 27,* 101-113.   [539
NBLiHi, NJQ.

O'Callaghan, Edmund B(ailey). Calendar of Historical Manuscripts in the Office of the Secretary of State, Albany, New York, 1865-6. Part I: Dutch MSS., 1630-1664; Part II, English MSS., 1664-1776.   [540
DLC, MBNEH, NBLiHi, NEh, NJQ, NN, NNNGB.

————— Calendar of New York colonial manuscripts, indorsed land papers, 1643-1803. 1864.   [541
DLC, NBLiHi, NN, NNNGB.

————— Marriage licenses, New York Province. In *New York Geneal. and Biog. Record, 1,* pp. 3, 13; *2,* pp. 25, 141, 194; *3,* pp. 91, 192; *4,* p. 31; *5,* p. 174.   [542
Az, C, CaOTP, CL, CoD, CSf, Ct, CtHi, CtY, DLC, DNDAR, IaHi, IC, ICN, ICU, In, MB, MBAt, MBNEH, MdBP, MeHi, MH, MHi, Mi, MiD-B, MNF, MnHi, MnM, MoK, MoS, MWA, N, NB, NBLiHi, NBu, NBuG, Nc, NEh, Nh, NHC, NHi, NIC, NjNbS, NjPla, NJQ, NN, NNC, NNNGB, NR, OC, OCHP, OCl, OClWHi, OHi, PEa, PEr, PHi, PPi, PPL, USlGS, Wa, WaS, WM.

————— The Documentary History of the State of New York. 4 vols. 1849-1851.   [543

This contains the following assessment, census, muster, rate and tax lists:

BROOKHAVEN town, Suffolk county
  Rate list, 1675: vol. II, pp. 468-469
  Rate list, 1683: vol. II, pp. 532-534

BROOKLYN town (Breuckelen), Kings county
  Assessment roll, August 20, 1675: vol. IV, pp. 144-150
  Assessment roll, September, 1676: vol. II, pp. 475-481
  Census, 1698: vol. III, pp 133-134
  List of inhabitants, 1738: vol. IV, pp. 195-198
  Valuation, September 26, 1683: vol. II, pp. 498-503

BUSHWICK town (Boswyck), Kings county
  Assessment roll, August 19, 1675: vol. IV, pp. 141-144
  Assessment roll, September 23, 1676: vol. II, pp. 482-485
  Census of 1698: vol. III, pp. 134-135
  List of inhabitants, 1738: vol. IV, pp. 198-200
  Rate list, September 8, 1683: vol. II, pp. 493-495

EAST HAMPTON town, Suffolk county
  Rate list, August 24, 1675: vol. II, pp. 441-442
  Rate list, 1683: vol. II, pp. 539-542

FLATBUSH town (Middelwout), Kings county
  Assessment roll, August 22, 1675: vol. IV, pp. 150-154
  Assessment roll, October 1, 1676: vol. II, pp. 470-475
  Census, 1698: vol. III, pp. 137-138
  List of inhabitants, 1738: vol. IV, pp. 188-191
  Rate list, 1683: vol. II, pp. 504-506

FLATLANDS town (Nieuw Amersfoort), Kings county
  Assessment roll, August 24, 1675: vol. IV, pp. 155-158
  Census, 1698: vol. III, p. 136
  List of inhabitants, 1738: vol. IV, pp. 191-192
  Rate list, September 25, 1683: vol. II, pp. 495-497
  Valuation, September, 1676: vol. II, pp. 485-488

FLUSHING town, Queens county
  List of inhabitants, (August) 1698: vol. I, pp. 661-665
  Rate list, September 29, 1683: vol. II, pp. 516-518
  Valuation, 1675: vol. II, p. 459-462

GRAVESEND town, Kings county
Census of 1698: vol. III, pp. 136-137
Patent to the town, 1645: vol. I, pp. 629-632
List of inhabitants, 1738: vol. IV, p. 193
Rate list, 1683: vol. II, pp. 508-511

HEMPSTEAD town, Queens county (now Nassau county)
Names of inhabitants, 1673: vol. I, p. 658
Rate list, October 11, 1683: vol. II, pp. 523-538

HUNTINGTON town, Suffolk county
Rate list, 1675: vol. II, pp. 443-446
Rate list, 1683: vol. II, p. 530

JAMAICA town, Queens county
Rate list, 1683: II, pp. 519-522

KINGS county
The roll of allegiance, 26 to 30 September, 1687: I, pp. 659-661
Militia list, 1715: vol. III, pp. 183-185

NEW UTRECHT town, Kings county
Assessment roll, August 24, 1675: vol. IV, pp. 158-160
Assessment roll, September 29, 1676: vol. II, pp. 485-488
Census of 1698: vol. III, pp. 135-136
Description of the founding of New Utrecht: vol. I, pp. 633-655
List of inhabitants, 1738: vol. IV, pp. 194-195
Rate list, September 28, 1683: vol. II, pp. 506-507

NEWTOWN town, Queens county
Rate list, September 1675: vol. II, pp. 464-467
Rate list, 1683: vol. II, pp. 512-515

OYSTER BAY town, Queens county (now Nassau county)
Rate list, September 29, 1683: vol. II, pp. 528-529

QUEENS county
List of the Queens county militia, 1738: vol. IV, pp. 209-210

SMITHTOWN town, Suffolk county
Rate list, September 28, 1683: vol. II, p. 531

SOUTHAMPTON town, Suffolk county
List of inhabitants, 1698: vol. I, pp. 665-669
Rate list, 1683: vol. II, pp. 536-538

SOUTHOLD town, Suffolk county
List of inhabitants, 1698: vol. I, pp. 669-673
Rate list, September 16, 1675: vol. II, pp. 447-448
Rate list, 1683: vol. II, pp. 535-536

SUFFOLK county
List of freeholders, February 27, 1737: vol. IV, p. 200
CtW, CU, DCU, DLC, DNDAR, DNW, IHi, InThE, MB, MBNEH, MdBP, MnH, MiU, MiU-C, N, NBLiHi, NcD, NcU, NEh, NIC, NiNbS, NjP, NJQ, NjR, NN, NNNGB, NWM, OCX, OClW, OU, PBMC, PP, PPT, PU, PV, PWcT, RWoU, TU, USlGS, ViU, WaU.

O'Connor, W. B. Bedford in Breuckelen town, 1667-1868. 1926. (Typed).
NBLiHi. [544

O'Gorman, William. Newtown records, published in the Newtown *Register*. 1934. (Typed.) [545
NBLiHi, NJQ.

———— Old Newtown: selections from the town scrap book, originally written by the town clerk. 1934. [546
NJQ (typed); NBLiHi (mounted clippings).

Old Bethpage, New York. Old Bethpage cemetery records. [547
NEh.

Onderdonk, Henry, jr. Tax lists of Flushing, 1784 and 1788. (MS and typed copy.)   [548

DLC, NBLiHi (manuscript).

Also published in the *Long Island Hist. Soc. Quarterly, 2,* pp. 81-87.

CoD, Ct, CtY, CU, DLC, DSI-M, ICN, IU, MeU, MH, MHi, MiD-B, MnHi, MWA, N, NB, NBB, NBLiHi, NBP, NBuG, NEh, NjP, NJQ, NN, NNC, OHi, PCA, PHi, VW, WaU, WHi.

————— The Annals of Hempstead; 1643 to 1832. 1878.   [549

DLC, DNDAR, MBNEH, MdBP, MWA, N, NBLiHi, NEh, NJQ, NN, NNNGB, NRvS, PHC, PHI, PPFr, PPM, USlGS.

————— Baptisms, St. George's Episcopal Church, Hempstead. Typed by Josephine C. Frost. 2 vols. (Typed.)   [550

NJQ.

————— Baptisms and marriages, St. George's Episcopal Church, Hempstead, New York. 1725-1845. (MS.)   [551

NBLiHi.

————— Census of Hempstead, 1698. (MS.)   [552

NBLiHi.

Also published in *New York Geneal. and Biog. Record, 45,* pp. 54-68.

Az, C, CaOTP, CL, CoD, CSf, Ct, CtHi, CtY, DLC, DNDAR, IaHi, IC, ICN, ICU, In, MB, MBAt, MBNEH, MdBP, MeHi, MH, MHi, Mi, MiD-B, MNF, MnHi, MnM, MoK, MoS, MWA, N, NB, NBLiHi, NBu, NBuG, Nc, NEh, Nh, NHC, NHi, NIC, NjNbS, NjPla, NJQ, NN, NNC, NNNGB, NR, OC, OCHP, OCl, OClWHi, OHi, PEa, PEr, PHi, PPi, PPL, USlGS, Wa, WaS, WM.

————— Tax lists of Hempstead, 1784, 1788, 1792 and 1797. (MS. and typed copy.)   [553

NBLiHi.

————— Records kept by the Rev. Thomas Poyer, rector of Episcopal churches at Jamaica and Flushing, New York. Typed by Josephine C. Frost. 1913.   [554

DLC, NBLiHi, NJQ, NN, NNNGB.

————— Account book of Aaron van Nostrand (chairmaker, 1767), sexton for grave digging, bell ringing, pall and attendings, at the Grace Episcopal Church of Jamaica, Long Island, New York, 1773-1820. Typed by Josephine C. Frost. 1913.   [555

DLC, NBLiHi, NJQ, PHi.

————— Early notes from Dutch churches at Newtown and Jamaica, Long Island; also, the inhabitants of Foster's Meadow in 1726. Copied from originals not extant, and typed by Josephine C. Frost.   [556

Includes officers of the Newtown Dutch Church, 1748-1834; members of the same, 1786-1834; and for the Jamaica Dutch Church: members, 1786-1835; also, owners of the burying ground, Foster's meadow, 1737.

NBLiHi, NJQ.

————— History of the First Reformed Dutch Church of Jamaica, Long Island. 1884.   [557

Refers to pastors, 1705-1877; officers, 1785-1884; members, 1715, 1786-1884, etc.

DLC, MWA, N, NB, NBLiHi, NEh, NJQ, NN, PHi.

———— Baptisms, marriages and funerals recorded at Grace Episcopal church, Jamaica, New York, 1769-1853. Typed by Josephine C. Frost. 1913. [558
DLC, NBLiHi, NJQ, USIGS.

———— Presbyterian church records, Jamaica, Long Island. Baptisms, 1679-1836 and marriages, 1775-1848. 2 vols. Typed by Josephine C. Frost. 1914. [559
NBLiHi, NJQ, NNNGB.

———— Jamaica tax lists, 1784, 1788. (MS. and typed copy.) [560
NBLiHi.

———— Bibliography of Long Island. In: *Antiquities of Long Island*, by Gabriel Furman. 1874. [561
DLC, MdBP, MH, MiU, MWA, N, NB, NBB, NBC, NBLiHi, NcU, NEh, NIC, NjN, NjP, NJQ, NN, NNC, NNNGB, OCIW, OClWHi, OU, PHi, PPM, PPPrHi.

———— Long Island and New York in olden times. 1851. [562
NBLiHi, NJQ, NN.

———— Births, marriages and deaths of Friends, copied out of the original by Isaac Horner as written in 1685. (MS.) [563
NBLiHi.

———— Manhasset (North Hempstead) Reformed Dutch Church records: Baptisms (1742-93); marriages (1785-1878) and deaths (1841-78). Typed by Josephine C. Frost. 1913. [564
DLC, MBNEH, NBLiHi, NJQ, NNNGB, USIGS. (MS at NBLiHi.)

———— Deaths from the Reformed Dutch Church at Manhasset, Long Island, 1790-1840. Copied from original records no longer in existence, and typed by Josephine C. Frost. 1913. [565
DLC, NBLiHi, NJQ, NNNGB, USIGS. (MS at NBLiHi.)

———— Marriages recorded at the Reformed Dutch Church, Manhasset, Long Island (formerly Success, then North Hempstead), 1785-1878 and 1826-1859; also a few deaths, 1841-1879. Typed by Josephine C. Frost. 1913. [566
DLC, MBNEH, NBLiHi, NEh, NJQ, NN.

———— Reformed Dutch Church of Manhasset. Minutes, 1731-1847. Typed by Josephine C. Frost. 1913. [567
NJQ.

———— Baptismal record of the Reformed Dutch Church at Newtown, Long Island, 1736 to 1846. Marriages by Rev. G. J. Garretson from 1835 to 1846. Typed by Josephine C. Frost. 1913. [568
DLC, MBNEH, NBLiHi, NJQ, NNNGB.

———— Tax lists of Newtown, 1786. (Typed.) [569
NBLiHi.

———— Baptismal records, 1741-1846 and marriages, 1826-1847 of the Reformed Dutch Church at Oyster Bay. Typed by Josephine C. Frost. [570
NBLiHi, NJQ, NNNGB.

———— Tax lists of Oyster Bay, 1784, 1788. (MS and typed copy.)
NBLiHi. [571

———— Queens County in olden times: being a supplement to the several histories thereof. 1865. [572
DLC, DNDAR, MBNEH, MH, MWA, N, NBLiHi, NEh, NIC, NJQ, NN, NNNGB, NSmB, PHi, PPL.

———— List of names in the old records of the several towns of Queens County; and list of names in Queens County records, 1722-1774. (MS.)
NBLiHi. [573

———— Documents and letters intended to illustrate the Revolutionary incidents of Queens County. First edition, 1846; second edition, 1884. [574
CaNSWA[1], DLC[1,2], DNR[1], I[2], MdBP[2], MH[1,2], MiU-C[2], MWA[1,2], N[1,2], NB[1], NBLiHi[1,2], NEh[2], NIC[1,2], NjP[1], NJQ[1,2], NN[1,2], NNC[1,2], NNNGB[1,2], NRvS[1,2], NSmB[2], OCl[1], OClWHi[2], PHi[1,2], PPL-R[1,2], PU[1].
Superscript numbers refer to edition.

———— Revolutionary incidents of Suffolk and Kings counties. First edition, 1849; second edition, 1884. [575
Both editions: CaNSWA, DLC, DNR, MBNEH, MdBP, MH, MWA, N, NB, NBLiHi, NEh, NIC, NjP, NJQ, NN, OCl, OClWHi, PHi, PPA; Second edition, PU.

———— History of the Society of Friends of the Westbury Meeting on Long Island. (MS.) [576
NBLiHi.

———— Diary, or dates of marriage and deaths of my family and friends, 1779-1859. (Hempstead, New York.) (MS. and typed copy.) [577
NBLiHi.

Order of Lords of Colonial Manors in America. Addresses delivered at annual meetings, etc. 30 pamphlets, 1916-1953 (variously bound and catalogued). [578
Included are: The Gardiner manor (1916), the Tangier Smith manor of St. George (1921), the Lloyd manor of Queens Village (1925), Shelter Island (1934), and Sagtikos manor (1935).
NBLiHi, NJQ, NNNGB.

Ostrander, Stephen M. A history of the city of Brooklyn and Kings County. 1894. [579
CU, ICU, N, NB, NBC, NBLiHi, NIC, NJQ, NN, NNC, NNNGB, OClWHi, TxU, USIGS.

Oyster Bay, New York. Cemeteries (Inscriptions), Oyster Bay. [580
Includes the Frost cemetery, Matinecock; Hegeman cemetery, Locust Valley; Rinnie Smith's farm cemetery, Selleck; Slade estate cemetery; Thomas Cock cemetery, Mill Neck; Valentine cemetery, Woodbury; Weeks cemetery, Lattingtown; Woolsey cemetery, Lattingtown; Wortman cemetery, Sand Hill Road in Oyster Bay.
NEh.

———— Papers relating to the town roads, 1796-1826. (MS.) [581
This includes a list of names in the western road district of the town.
NJQ.

———— Cape Codders: first white folk to live in Oyster Bay. Five articles from the Oyster Bay *Enterprise-Pilot*. Mounted.   [582 NBLiHi.

———— Friends' cemetery in Oyster Bay, New York. (Inscriptions.) NJQ.   [583

Pantle, Alberta. List of ships belonging to Sag Harbor employed in whale fishing. (From the *New England Almanac, 1845-1856*). (MS.) Names captains and owners.   [584 NBLiHi.

Parcells, Elsie (Hoxie) (Mrs. Frank H.) Inscriptions from the Cornwall family cemetery at Sands Point, New York. 1934. (Typed.)   [585 NBLiHi.

———— Births and Marriages from the town records of Southampton. Births, 1660-1778; Marriages 1660-1768. In *Daughters of the American Revolution Magazine, 87*, pp. 409-412; 1,247-1,249.   [586 CtU, DLC, DNDAR, ICN, InI, KyLoF, MiD-B, MiGr, MnHi, MoS, NBLiHi, NEh, Nh, NN, NNNGB, OCl, OClWHi, OY, PPi, T, Vi, WHi.

———— Inscriptions in the South End burying ground, Southampton. In *Daughters of the American Revolution Magazine, 87*, pp. 1,249-1,250.
                                                                          [587 CtU, DLC, DNDAR, ICN, InI, KyLoF, MiD-B, MiGr, MnHi, MoS, NBLiHi, NEh, Nh, NN, NNNGB, OCl, OClWHi, OY, PPi, T, Vi, WHi.

Patchogue, New York, Chamber of Commerce. Directory of Patchogue, Long Island. 1926.   [588 NEh.

Patten, J. Alexander. Lives of the clergy of New York and Brooklyn; embracing two hundred biographies of eminent living men in all denominations. Also the list out of each sect and congregation. Atlantic Publishing Company, 1874. Another edition: E. Walker's Sons, bookmakers, New York, 1878.   [589 MBNEH.

Payne, E. B. Justice of the Peace. Criminal dockets for 1895-1903. (Riverhead, New York.) (MS.)   [590 NJQ.

Peck, Theodore M. St. John's Church, Huntington, New York. Personal record of Theodore M. Peck, pastor, 1884-1892. Marriages, baptisms, etc. 3 vols. (MS.)   [591 NJQ.

Pelletreau, William S(mith). Early Long Island Wills of Suffolk County, 1691-1703. 1897.   [592 DLC, DNDAR, MB, MBNEH, MdBP, MH, MWA, N, NBLiHi, NcD, NEh, NHu, NIC, NJQ, NN, NNNGB, NSmB, OClWHi, PHi, USlGS.

———— Wills of the Smith families of New York and Long Island, 1664-1794, abstracted.   1898.   [593
DLC, DNDAR, MB, MBNEH, NBLiHi, NEh, NJQ, NN, NNNGB.

———— Smithtown, Long Island: Records of the Town.   1898.   [594
CtY, CU, DLC, DNDAR, MB, MBNEH, N, NBLiHi, NEh, NJQ, NN, NNNGB, NSmB, USlGS.

———— A complete list of all the brownstone and slate tombstone inscriptions in the North End burying ground, Southampton, Long Island. In *New York Geneal. and Biog. Record, 2*, p. 31; *46*, p. 19.   [595
Az, C, CaOTP, CL, CoD, CSf, Ct, CtHi, CtY, DLC, DNDAR, IaHi, IC, ICN, ICU, In, MB, MBAt, MBNEH, MdBP, MeHi, MH, MHi, Mi, MiD-B, MNF, MnHi, MnM, MoK, MoS, MWA, N, NB, NBLiHi, NBu, NBuG, Nc, NEh, Nh, NHC, NHi, NIC, NjNbS, NjPla, NJQ, NN, NNC, NNNGB, NR, OC, OCHP, OCl, OClWHi, OHi, PEa, PEr, PHi, PPi, PPL, USlGS, Wa. WaS, WM.

———— History of Suffolk County, with illustrations, portraits and sketches of prominent families and individuals.   (W. W. Munsell and Co.)   1882.   [596
DLC, DNDAR, MBNEH, MWA, N, NBLiHi, NEh, NHu, NHuHi, NIC, NJQ, NN, NNNGB, NSmB, USlGS.
(See also No. 516.)

Pelletreau, William S(mith) and J. H. Brown.   American families of historic lineage.   Long Island edition.   2 vols.   [597
NBLiHi, NEh, NN.

Pennypacker, F(rank) Morton.   Articles relating to Long Island history and genealogy, contributed to the *Brooklyn Daily Eagle*, 1928-1930.   (Clippings, mounted.)   [598
The clippings were prepared by Hazel Griffin.
NBLiHi, NEh, NN.

———— Presbyterian Church records of East Hampton, 1696-1884; extract from the printed records of the town, Vol. 5, with typewritten additions.   [599
NN.

Perris, William.   Maps of the city of Brooklyn, 1855.   2 vols.   2nd ed., 1860/61.   2 vols.   [600
NBLiHi.

Perris, William and J. H. Higginson.   Plan of the city of Brooklyn showing the ancient farm boundaries.   1855.   [601
NBLiHi.

Perry, Dr. Stephen.   Records of births and deaths in an account book of Northport, 1881-1885.   Copied by Edna Huntington.   1938.   (Typed.)   [602
NBLiHi, NJQ.

Petty, Joseph H.   Abstracts of wills from New York Surrogate's office, relating to families of Brookhaven.   In *New York Geneal. and Biog. Record, 11*, p. 24; *12*, p. 46; *14*, p. 140; *24*, pp. 88, 142.   [603

Az, C, CaOTP, CL, CoD, CSf, Ct, CtHi, CtY, DLC, DNDAR, IaHi, IC, ICN, ICU, In, MB, MBAt, MBNEH, MdBP, MeHi, MH, MHi, Mi, MiD-B, MNF, MnHi, MnM, MoK, MoS, MWA, N, NB, NBLiHi, NBu, NBuG, Nc, NEh, Nh, NHC, NHi, NIC, NjNbS, NjPla, NJQ, NN, NNC, NNNGB, NR, OC, OCHP, OCl, OClWHi, OHi, PEa, PEr, PHi, PPi, PPL, USlGS, Wa, WaS, WM.
NNNGB, Original MS.

———— Original deeds and land transactions in East Hampton . . . involving the Huntting, Mulford and allied families. (MS.) [604
NNNGB.

———— Records of the Presbyterian Church in Mattituck . . . 1751-1776; also inscriptions from the churchyard and marriages performed. 1847-1890. (MS.) [605
NNNGB.

Phelps-Stokes, I. N. The Iconography of Manhattan Island, 1498-1909. 1915-1928. 6 vols. [606
Contains references to early settlers of Kings County.
DLC, NBLiHi, NEh, NN, NNNGB.

Platt, Major Epenetus. Miscellaneous papers, 1705-1737. (Huntington.)
NHi. [607

Platt, Henry C(lay). Old times in Huntington . . . with additional notes and family sketches. 1876. [608
CSmH, DLC, MWA, N, NBLiHi, NEh, NHu, NHuHi, NjP, NJQ, NN, NNC, NNNGB, NRvS, NSmB, PHi.

Polk's Directories. Polk's (Trow's) directories for: [609
Freeport, New York. Vol. 1, 1923/24; 1930/31.
Glen Cove, New York. Vol. 1, 1923/24.
Hempstead, New York. Vol. 1, 1923/24; vol. 3, 1930/31.
Lynbrook, New York. 1928/29.
Queens and Richmond counties, New York. Vol. 1, 1933/34.
Rockville Centre, New York. 1923/24; 1926/27.
NJQ, NN (Queens and Richmond only).

Post, Richard H. Notes on Quogue, 1659-1959. 1959. [610
NBLiHi, NEh, NJQ.

Powell, Edgar. Directory of Great Neck, Manhasset and Plandome, New York. 1924. [611
MWA, NN.

Poyer, Rev. Thomas. Jamaica, New York (Episcopalian) parish registers, 1710-1732. In *New York Geneal. and Biog. Record, 19*, pp. 5, 53. [612
Az, C, CaOTP, CL, CoD, CSf, Ct, CtHi, CtY, DLC, DNDAR, IaHi, IC, ICN, ICU, In, MB, MBAt, MBNEH, MdBP, MeHi, MH, MHi, Mi, MiD-B, MNF, MnHi, MnM, MoK, MoS, MWA, N, NB, NBLiHi, NBu, NBuG, Nc, NEh, Nh, NHC, NHi, NIC, NjNbS, NjPla, NJQ, NN, NNC, NNNGB, NR, OC, OCHP, OCl, OClWHi, OHi, PEa, PEr, PHi, PPi, PPL, USlGS, Wa, WaS, WM.

Prime, Nathaniel Scudder. History of Long Island. 1845. [613
DLC, MB, MdBP, MH, MWA, N, NB, NBC, NBLiHi, NEh, NHu, NIC, NjN, NjNbS, NjP, NJQ, NN, NNC, NNNGB, NRvS, NSmB, OClWHi.

Promised Land, New York. Cemeteries (inscriptions). In *Long Island Life,* vol. 7-8, 1918-1919.   [614
NJQ.

Provost, Andrew Jackson, jr. Early settlers of Bushwick, Long Island, New York and their descendants. 1952-1960. 3 vols.   [615
DLC, DNDAR, MBNEH, NBLiHi, NEh, NJQ, NN, NNNGB (vol. 1), USIGS.

Purcell, Edith M. Across the years; the story of Floral Park, New York. 1958.   [616
DLC, NJQ, NBLiHi, NN.

Queens county and borough, New York. Historical miscellany on persons, houses, etc. "History map of the Borough of Queens".   [617
NNNGB (microfilm).

——————— Abstracts of deeds, Queens County, New York. Libers A to D (1683-1785). (Typed.) Liber E (1764-1788). (MS.)   [618
MWA (libers A-D), NBLiHi (libers A-D), NJQ (libers A-E), NNNGB (libers A-D, microfilm).

——————— Queens County local papers, 1720-1822. 1 folder.   [619
NHi.

——————— Papers of the Queens County militia, 1761-1785.   [620
NEh (originals); NN (Manuscript Room).

——————— Abstracts of early wills of Queens County, recorded in libers A and C of Deeds in the Register's office at Jamacia, and for 1683-1744. (Typed.)   [621
NJQ, USIGS.

——————— Cock-Cocks family papers of Queens County and Oyster Bay, 1724-1818. (MS.)   [622
NN.

Queens County Loan Officers. Liber D, pp. 624-747 for 1754-1760. Mortgages for loans made to residents of Queens County. (MS.)   [623
NJQ.

Quogue, New York. Cemeterv inscriptions and records of the Presbyterian Church at Quogue. (MS.)   [624
NNNGB.

Rattray, Jeannette (Edwards). East Hampton history, including genealogies of early families. 1953.   [625
DLC, DNDAR, MBNEH, NBLiHi, NEh, NJQ, NN, NNNGB, USIGS.

Republican Watchman. Births, marriages and deaths from the *Republican Watchman,* 1867-1901. (Mounted clippings.)   [626
NBLiHi, NEh.

Reynolds' Directories. Directory of the city of Williamsburgh, 1847/48, 1848/49, 1851/52, 1853, 1854.   [627
The directory for 1851/52 includes a history of the city of Williamsburgh, by Samuel Reynolds.
MWA, NB, NBLiHi, NJQ, NN.

Reynolds, Cuyler. Genealogical and family history of Southern New York and the Hudson river valley. 1913. 3 vols. [628
DLC, DNGS (vol. III), DNDAR, MBNEH, NBLiHi, NEh, NJQ, NN, NNNGB.

Richardson, James F. Historical account and inventory of records of Suffolk County. 1921. [629
DLC, N, NBLiHi, NJQ, NN, NSmB.

Richmond, F. A., and Co. Flushing village directory, 1887/88. [630
MWA, NN.

Richmond Hill Record. Directory of Richmond Hill. Morris Park, Brooklyn Manor, Woodhaven, Ozone Park, Forest Park, Union Course and vicinity. 1910. [631
NJQ.

Righter, S. Ward. List of freeholders of Smithtown, 1810-1820. In *New York Geneal. and Biog. Record, 56,* p. 102. [632
Az, C, CaOTP, CL, CoD, CSf, Ct, CtHi, CtY, DLC, DNDAR, IaHi, IC, ICN, ICU, In, MB, MBAt, MBNEH, MdBP, MeHi, MH, MHi, Mi, MiD-B, MNF, MnHi, MnM, MoK, MoS, MWA, N, NB, NBLiHi, NBu, NBuG, Nc, NEh, Nh, NHC, NHi, NIC, NjNbS, NjPla, NJQ, NN, NNC, NNNGB, NR, OC, OCHP, OCl, OClWHi, OHi, PEa, PEr, PHi, PPi, PPL, USlGS, Wa, WaS, WM.

Riker, James. The Annals of Newtown in Queens County, New York. 1852. With genealogies of early families. [633
DLC, DNDAR, MBNEH, MdBP, MWA, N, NB, NBLiHi, NcD, NEh, NHu, NIC, NjNbS, NJQ, NN, NNC, NNNGB, NSmB, PHi, PPL, PPPrHi, USlGS.
The personal copy of James Riker, with additional information, is in NJQ.

———— Historical notes of Newtown. Copied from the James Riker papers in the manuscript room of the New York City Public Library. 4 vols. (Typed.) [634
NJQ.

———— The Riker manuscripts. (MS.) [635
This relates to families of Kings and Queens counties, partly unpublished.
NN (Manuscript Room), NNNGB (microfilm).

Riverhead, New York. Riverhead Congregational Church records. Baptisms, 1838-1901; deaths, 1839-1918; marriages, 1871-1901; lists of members. (MS.) [636
NBLiHi.

Robbins, William A(lfred). Brookhaven, New York, census, 1810, 1850. (MS.) [637
NBLiHi.

———— Burying ground north of Alker mansion, Great Neck. 1905. (Typed.) [638
NBLiHi.

———— Inscriptions in the Tredwell burying ground, Great Neck. In *Long Island Hist. Soc. Quarterly, 1,* p. 12. [639
CoD, Ct, CtY, CU, DLC, DSI-M, ICN, IU, MeU, MH, MHi, MiD-B, MnHi, MWA, N, NB, NBB, NBLiHi, NBP, NBuG, NEh, NjP, NJQ, NN, NNC, OHi, PCA, PHi, VW, WaU, WHi.

——————— Index of deeds, Huntington, Long Island, 1669-1789. (Typed.)
NBLiHi.   [640

——————— Marriages, baptisms and deaths, 1766-1817, in the Presbyterian
Church at Huntington.   (Typed.)   [641
NBLiHi.

——————— Old Cemetery at Huntington.   (On cards.)   [642
NBLiHi.

——————— 1810 census of Islip.   (Typed.)   [643
NBLiHi.

——————— Marriages in the Methodist Protestant Church by Rev. George
H. Jackson at Lynbrook.   1826-1827.   (Typed.)   [644
NBLiHi.

——————— Riverhead, New York, tombstone inscriptions.   (On cards.) [645
NBLiHi.

——————— Inscriptions from a private burial ground in St. James.   1930.
NBLiHi.   [646

——————— The Methodist churchyard at Selden.   (Inscriptions.)   1937.
(Typed.)   [647
NBLiHi.

——————— Smithtown, New York, First Presbyterian Church records.   In
New York Geneal. and Biog. Record, 44, pp. 279, 384; *45,* p. 8.   [648
Az, C, CaOTP, CL, CoD, CSf, Ct, CtHi, CtY, DLC, DNDAR, IaHi, IC, ICN, ICU,
In, MB, MBAt, MBNEH, MdBP, MeHi, MH, MHi, Mi, MiD-B, MNF, MnHi, MnM,
MoK, MoS, MWA, N, NB, NBLiHi, NBu, NBuG, Nc, NEh, Nh, NHC, NHi, NIC,
NjNbS, NjPla, NJQ, NN, NNC, NNNGB, NR, OC, OCHP, OCl, OClWHi, OHi,
PEa, PEr, PHi, PPi, PPL, USlGS, Wa. WaS, WM.

——————— Partial list of inscriptions from the burying ground of the Presbyterian Church at Smithtown.   (Typed.)   [649
NBLiHi.

——————— Vital Records, Southold, New York.   In *New York Geneal. and
Biog. Record, 47,* p. 344; *48,* pp. 20, 79, 164, 275, 341; *49,* pp. 64, 154,
265.   [650
Az, C, CaOTP, CL, CoD, CSf, Ct, CtHi, CtY, DLC, DNDAR, IaHi, IC, ICN, ICU, In,
MB, MBAt, MBNEH, MdBP, MeHi, MH, MHi, Mi, MiD-B, MNF, MnHi, MnM, MoK,
MoS, MWA, N, NB, NBLiHi, NBu, NBuG, Nc, NEh, Nh, NHC, NHi, NIC, NjNbS,
NjPla, NJQ, NN, NNC, NNNGB, NR, OC, OCHP, OCl, OClWHi, OHi, PEa, PEr,
PHi, PPi, PPL, USlGS, Wa, WaS, WM.

——————— The Salmon Records, Southold, New York.   [651
DLC, DNDAR, MBNEH, MWA, N, NBLiHi (with MS additions and corrections).
NEh, NJQ, NN, NNNGB, USlGS.

——————— Genealogical notes, families of Suffolk County.   (On cards.)
NBLiHi.   [652

——————— Index of names, Book A of Deeds, Suffolk County, 1686-1719.
(MS.)   [653
NBLiHi.

Robbins, William A(lfred) and Georgia G. Cockcroft. Brookhaven cemeteries. 1929/31. (Typed.) [654

Coram-Mt. Sinai Road: Bayles plot.
Holtsville: Two cemeteries.
Lake Grove: Hawkins plot.
Lake Ronkonkoma: Methodist churchyard and adjoining cemetery; cemetery on St. James Road.
Mt. Sinai: Davis plot.
Patchogue: Lakeside cemetery.
Selden: Hallock and Poe plots.
Setauket-Ronkonkoma Road: Hawkins plot.
Setauket: Presbyterian cemetery.
Stony Brook: Rudyard, Smith, and Davis-Hallock plots.
NBLiHi.

———— Commack Methodist Episcopal graveyard. Inscriptions. 1938. (Typed.) [655

NBLiHi.

———— Hauppauge Methodist Episcopal Church cemetery. Inscriptions. 1928. (Typed.) [656

NBLiHi.

Roberts, William Willard. Pioneers and patriots of Long Island, 1640-1840. 1936. [657

DLC, MS, MWA, NBLiHi, NEh, NHu, NHuHi, NN, PP.

Robinson, Elisha. Atlas of Kings County, compiled from official records, private plans and actual surveys. 1890. [658

DLC, N, NB, NBLiHi, NJQ, NN.

———— Atlas of the city of Brooklyn, embracing all territory within its corporate limits; from official records, private plans and actual surveys. 1886. [659

DLC, NB, NBLiHi, NJQ, NN.

———— Atlas of the 29th, 30th, 31st and 32nd wards (formerly towns of Flatbush, New Utrecht, Gravesend and Flatlands, Kings County), borough of Brooklyn, city of New York; from official records, private plans and actual surveys. 1898. [660

DLC, N, NB, NBLiHi, NN.

———— Certified copies of important maps of Wards 8, 17, 18, 21, 22, 23, 24 and 25, city of Brooklyn, filed in the Office of Register, Kings County. 1889. [661

DLC, NJQ, NN.

Robinson's Directories. Garden City, 1937/38, 1946; Great Neck, 1937/8, 1946/47; Manhasset and Plandome, 1938; Floral Park, 1937/38, 1938/39; Hempstead, 1935/36, 1938/39; Little Neck, 1938/39; and Mineola, 1940, directories. [662

NJQ.

Rogers, Beatrice G. Historical sketch of the incorporated village of Westhampton Beach, 1640-1951. [663

NJQ, NN.

Ronk, Daniel T. First Reformed Church of Brooklyn. Tombstone inscriptions copied from their lot in Greenwood cemetery. 1920. (Typed.)
NN.   [664

Ross, Peter. A history of Long Island, from its earliest settlement to the present time. 1902. 3 vols.   [665
DLC, DNDAR, MWA, NB, NBC, NBLiHi, NEh, NHu, NHuHi, NIC, NJQ, NN, NNC, NNNGB, NSmB, OCl, OO, PHi, USlGS.

Ross, Peter, and William S. Pelletreau. A history of Long Island.
3 vols. 1903.   [666
NBLiHi, NN.

Ryerson, Albert W(inslow). Inscriptions from two old cemeteries in Flushing. 1911. (Typed.)   [667
NBLiHi, NNNGB.

———— Long Island gravestone inscriptions. (Typed.)   [668
Private cemeteries at North Beach, on Black Stump Road, two and one-half miles from Flushing (Brinkerhoff).
NBLiHi.

Sag Harbor, New York. Cemetery inscriptions, Sag Harbor. In *New York Geneal. and Biog. Record, 2, 30.*   [669
Az, C, CaOTP, CL, CoD, CSf, Ct, CtHi, CtY, DLC, DNDAR, IaHi, IC, ICN, ICU, In, MB, MBAt, MBNEH, MdBP, MeHi, MH, MHi, Mi, MiD-B, MNF, MnHi, MnM, MoK, MoS, MWA, N, NB, NBLiHi, NBu, NBuG, Nc, NEh, Nh, NHC, NHi, NIC, NjNbS, NjPla, NJQ, NN, NNC, NNNGB, NR, OC, OCHP, OCl, OClWHi, OHi, PEa, PEr, PHi, PPi, PPL, USlGS, Wa, WaS, WM.

Sag Harbor Express. Inscriptions from the North Side burying ground, Sag Harbor. In the *Sag Harbor Express,* 29 June 1911. (Mounted clippings.)   [670
NBLiHi.

Sag Harbor, New York. Trustees' journal, old Sag Habor burying ground, 1845-1870. (MS.)   [671
NBLiHi.

———— Vital records of the Presbyterian Church, Sag Harbor, from 1791 to 1914. 1940.   [672
NEh.

———— Records of school district No. 11 of the town of Southampton in the village of Sag Harbor, 1819-1862. 2 vols. (MS.)   [673
Contains names of parents and number of children in each family.
NBLiHi.

Sammis, Romanah. The records of Huntington, Suffolk County. 1921.
                                                                          [674
DLC, N, NBLiHi, NEh, NJQ, NN, NNC, NNNGB, NSmB, OClWHi.

———— Huntington-Babylon town history. 1937.   [675
DLC, MBNEH, MWA, N, NBLiHi, NEh, NJQ, NN, NNNGB, NSmB.

Sandy, B. H. C. and Co. Complete ward atlas of Brooklyn, containing complete maps of each ward and of the town of Flatbush, shown on separate sheets arranged numerically. 1892. [676
NBLiHi.

Sawyer, Ray C(owen). Deaths published in the *Christian Intelligencer* of the Reformed Dutch Church from 1830 to 1871, which took place in Brooklyn and Long Island. [677
DLC, NBLiHi, NN.

———— Marriages published in the *Christian Intelligencer* of the Reformed Dutch church from 1830 to 1871, which took place in Brooklyn and Long Island. 1933. 10 vols. (Typed.) [678
DLC, DNDAR, MBNEH, NBLiHi, NJQ, NN, NNNGB.

———— Index of New York wills, 1662-1850, on file at the office of the Surrogate for New York County, in the Hall of Records, New York City, N. Y. 1932. 2 vols. (Typed.) [679
MWA, N, NBLiHi, NN.

———— Abstracts of wills, Queens County, subsequent to 1787, on file in the County Clerk's office at Jamaica. 1934. [680
The title varies. The 4 volumes to 1813 were issued in 1934; the series was later carried to 1850.
DLC, DNDAR, MBNEH, NBLiHi, NJQ, NNNGB (microfilm), USIGS.

Schoonmaker, Rev. Jacob. Marriages performed at Jamaica. 1803-1851. Copied by Henry Onderdonk, Jr., about 1851. Typed by Josephine C. Frost. [681
NBLiHi.

Schoonmaker, Dr. Martinus. Flatbush, New York. Baptisms, 1802-1847. Typed by Frances Bergen Cropsey. [682
NBLiHi.

Schubel, George. Illustrated history of greater Ridgewood, New York. 1913. [683
Includes biographies of residents.
NBLiHi, NJQ, NN.

Schultz, Bernice. Colonial Hempstead. [684
DLC, MWA, N, NBC, NBLiHi, NEh, NJQ, NN, NNNGB, NSmB.

Scudder, Moses L. Records of the First Church, Huntington, New York, being the record kept by the Rev. Ebenezer Prime: 1723-1779. 1899. [685
DLC, MBNEH, N, NBLiHi, NHu, NHuHi, NJQ, NN, NNNGB, NSmB, USIGS.

Scudder, Nellie (Ritch), and others. Manuscripts relating chiefly to families of Huntington, New York, including Babylon. (MS.) [686
NHuHi.

Sealock, Richard B. and Pauline A. Sealey.   Long Island Bibliography. 1940.   [687
CSmH, CU, DLC, ICJ, NBC, NBLiHi, NEh, NN, ICl, OFH, OU.

Setauket, New York.   Setauket gravestone inscriptions.   (The Smith burying ground.)   In *Long Island Hist. Soc. Quarterly*, 1, pp. 1-81. [688
CoD, Ct, CtY, CU, DLC, DSI-M, ICN, IU, MeU, MH, MHi, MiD-B, MnHi, MWA, N, NB, NBB, NBLiHi, NBP, NBuG, NEh, NjP, NJQ, NN, NNC, OHi, PCA, PHi, VW, WaU, WHi.

———— Marriage, burial and baptismal records of the Caroline Episcopal Church at Setauket, New York, 1822-1916.   [689
NEh.

Seversmith, Herbert Furman.   Colonial families of Long Island, New York and Connecticut.   (Offset.)   4 vols.   1944-1955.   [690
C, CL, Ct, DLC, DNDAR (microfilm), DNGS (1-3 microfilm, 4), ICN, MB, MBNEH, MiD, MnHi, MoStj, N, NBLiHi, NEh, NHuHi, NjHi, NJQ, NN, NNHol (microfilm), OClWHi (microfilm), PHi, USlGS.

Shaw, Osborn.   Brookhaven Town Cemetery Book.   [691
(This is a compilation of inscriptions in all the cemeteries in the town of Brookhaven, New York, that were known to Mr. Shaw, after many years of search.)
BELLE TERRE: Old slave and traditionally Indian graveyard.
BELLPORT: Col. William Howell private cemetery; Munsell private cemetery; Old Bellport cemetery; Woodland cemetery; Woodruff private cemetery, East Bellport.
BLUE POINT: Avery private cemetery (all stones removed to the Blue Point cemetery); Blue Point cemetery (formerly Methodist).
BROOKHAVEN (village): Barteau private cemetery; Brookhaven (Fireplace) village cemetery; Corwin private cemetery; Fireplace Methodist cemetery; Azel Hawkins private cemetery; David Hawkins private cemetery; Nathaniel Hawkins private cemetery; "King David" Hulse private cemetery; Ketcham private cemetery; Miller private cemetery; Post private cemetery (all stones removed to the Woodland cemetery, Bellport); Rose private cemetery No. 1, Rose private cemetery No. 2 (stones removed to the Brookhaven village cemetery).
CANAAN LAKE, North Patchogue: Wickes private cemetery.
CENTEREACH: Isaac Hammond private cemetery; George Lie private cemetery.
CENTRE MORICHES: Bishop and Reeve private cemetery; Bishop and Robinson private cemetery; Isaac Bishop private cemetery; Solomon Bishop private cemetery; Duryea private cemetery (stones removed to the Babylon, New York Rural cemetery); Gardiner private cemetery; Methodist cemetery; Mount Pleasant cemetery; New Presbyterian cemetery; Old Presbyterian cemetery; Abraham Osborn and Elisha Raynor private cemetery; A. M. E. Zion church cemetery.
CORAM: Bayles private cemetery; Coram village cemetery (New Methodist); Elijah Davis private cemetery; Old Baptist cemetery; Jonah Smith cemetery; Still private cemetery.
EAST MANORVILLE: David Robinson private cemetery.
EAST MORICHES: Col. Josiah Smith and Howell private cemetery.
EAST PATCHOGUE: Hedges and Osborn private cemetery; Hurtin private cemetery (all stones removed to Patchogue, New York); Overton private cemetery; Robinson private cemetery; Roe private cemetery (all stones removed to Cedar Grove cemetery, Patchogue, New York); Smith private cemetery.
EAST SETAUKET: Hulse private cemetery (some stones have been removed to the Baker private cemetery at Patchogue, New York); Strong private cemetery.
HOLTSVILLE: Waverly-Holtsville cemetery.
LAKE GROVE: Hallock private cemetery; Lakeville Rural cemetery (Methodist); Newton and L'Hommedieu private cemetery; Nicols private cemetery.
LAKE GROVE-CENTEREACH: New Village Congregational church cemetery.
LAKE RONKONKOMA: James and Israel Smith private cemetery (on the Maude Adams property).

MANORVILLE: "Cherry Valley", Hallock and Homan private cemetery; Lane and Terry private cemetery; Methodist cemetery; Old Presbyterian cemetery; Raynor private cemetery; Job Raynor private cemetery; Joseph Raynor private cemetery; Robinson and Gordon private cemetery; Stanborough private cemetery; Wines private cemetery.

MASTIC: Poosepattuck Indian and Negro cemetery; Nicoll Floyd private graveyard; Woodhull-Nicoll-Lawrence private cemetery.

MIDDLE ISLAND: Brewster private cemetery; Dayton private cemetery; Methodist cemetery; Union cemetery and the same, northern part.

MILLERS PLACE: Davis and Miller private cemetery; Miller private cemetery; Andrew Miller private cemetery.

MOUNT SINAI: Davis private cemetery; Eliakim Davis private cemetery; Joseph Davis private cemetery; Samuel Davis private cemetery; Sea View cemetery of the first Congregational church of Brookhaven; Ancient Hopkins private cemetery in Pipe Stave Hollow; Petty private cemetery; Phillips and Davis private cemetery; Tooker private cemetery at Crystal Brook.

NORTH MASTIC: Lane private cemetery at Paineville.

PATCHOGUE: Baker private cemetery (stones moved to Cedar Grove cemetery, Patchogue); Catholic cemetery; Cedar Grove cemetery; Lake View cemetery (Episcopal) of West Patchogue; Patchogue Union cemetery (Old Patchogue village cemetery at West Patchogue); Rice cemetery adjoining Lake View cemetery; Roe and Miller private cemetery (all stones removed to Cedar Grove cemetery); Ananias Smith private cemetery (remains reinterred in Cedar Grove cemetery).

PORT JEFFERSON: Drown Meadow or Port Jefferson Methodist cemetery (all stones removed to Cedar Hill cemetery, Echo, Port Jefferson); John Roe senior private cemetery (all stones removed to Cedar Hill cemetery); Cedar Hill cemetery at Echo.

RIDGE: Longwood (Tangier) Smith private cemetery; Stephen Randall private cemetery.

ROCKY POINT: Noah Hallock private cemetery at Hallock's Landing; Jones private cemetery.

SELDEN: Longbotham private cemetery; Norton private cemetery; Capt. Daniel Roe private cemetery; Joseph Ruland private cemetery; Selden Union cemetery (formerly a Norton private graveyard).

SETAUKET: John Biggs private cemetery; Joseph Brewster private cemetery; Caroline Episcopal church cemetery and the same, northern part; First Presbyterian church cemetery of Brookhaven; Laurel Hill Negro cemetery; Methodist cemetery; Arthur Smith private cemetery; Col. William (Tangier) Smith and Strong private cemetery at Strong's Neck; Jonathan Thompson private cemetery.

SHOREHAM: Sell private cemetery.

SMITH'S POINT: Judge William (Tangier) Smith's private cemetery.

SOUTH HAVEN: Samuel Carman and Nathaniel Miller private cemetery; Homan private cemetery; South Haven Presbyterian church cemetery.

SOUTH SETAUKET: Hawkins private ground at Nassakeage.

STONY BROOK: Bethel Negro cemetery; Jonas Davis private cemetery (now included with the Woods and Hallock private cemetery); "Quaker" Hallock private cemetery; Methodist cemetery; Oak Hill cemetery; Smith and Rudyard private cemetery; Woods and Hallock private cemetery.

SWEZEYTOWN: Swezey and Edwards private cemetery.

WADING RIVER: Tuthill private cemetery at West Wading River (stones removed to Sea View cemetery, Mount Sinai).

WEST MORICHES: Fanning private cemetery; Joseph Hawkins private cemetery; William Hawkins and Daniel Downs private cemetery; Negro cemetery.

WEST WADING RIVER: Robinson private cemetery, Long Chestnuts.

YAPHANK: Robert Hawkins private cemetery; Homan and Buckingham private cemetery; Old Baptist cemetery; Presbyterian church cemetery; St. Andrews Episcopal church cemetery; Cemetery of the Suffolk county Alms House; Yaphank village cemetery; Small private cemetery west of Yaphank ave., Yaphank and Brookhaven village.

TOWN CLERK'S OFFICE, PATCHOGUE, NEW YORK.

———— Documents of the town of Brookhaven, 1693-1947.   [692

NJQ.

———— Minutes of the Committee of Safety, town of Brookhaven; Manor of St. George and Patentship of Moriches. Typed by Edna Huntington. 1913.   [693
NBLiHi.

Sherman, Franklin J. Building up greater Queens Borough. 1929.   [694
Includes biographies.
NBLiHi, NJQ, NN.

Skillman, Francis. Some notes relating to Roslyn. 1829-1864.   (MS.)
NBLiHi.   [695

Sleight, Harry D. Sag Harbor in earlier days. 1930.   [696
Includes early censuses, school registers, etc.
NJQ.

———— Town records of the Town of Smithtown, Long Island, N. Y. 1837-1925. 2 vols.   [697
NBLiHi, NIC, NJQ.

Smith, Mrs. George Wilson. Upper Aquebogue, L. I., cemetery registry; Jamesport, L. I. (Lower Aquebogue) cemetery register. In *New York Geneal. and Biog. Record, 38,* pp. 305, 309.   [698
Az, C, CaOTP, CL, CoD, CSf, Ct, CtHi, CtY, DLC, DNDAR, IaHi, IC, ICN, ICU, In, MB, MBAt, MBNEH, MdBP, MeHi, MH, MHi, Mi, MiD-B, MNF, MnHi, MnM, MoK, MoS, MWA, N, NB, NBLiHi, NBu, NBuG, Nc, NEh, Nh, NHC, NHi, NIC, NjNbS, NjPla, NJQ, NN, NNC, NNNGB, NR, OC, OCHP, OCl, OClWHi, OHi, PEa, PEr, PHi, PPi, PPL, USlGS, Wa, WaS, WM.

Smith, Leroy. Marriages, Cutchogue, New York, 1787-1797.   In *The Amer. Genealogist, 18,* p. 118.   [699
CL, CoD, Ct, CtHi, CtY, DLC, DNGS, ICN, In, KHi, MB, MPB, MWA, MeBa, MeHi, Mi, MiD-B, MnHi, MoS, N, NBuG, NJQ, NN, NR, OC, OCHP, OCl, OClWHi, OHi, PEr, PHi, VW, WHi, WaSp.

———— Middle Island Presbyterian Church. Marriages, 1818-1862. In *The American Genealogist, 19,* p. 110.   [700
CL, CoD, Ct, CtHi, CtY, DLC, DNGS, ICN, In, KHi, MB, MBP, MWA, MeBa, MeHi, Mi, MiD-B MnHi, MoS, N, NBuG, NJQ, NN, NR, OC, OCHP, OCl, OClWHi, OHi, PEr, PHi, VW, WHi, WaSp.

Snyder, John J. Tales of old Flatbush. 1945.   [701
DLC, NBC, NBLiHi, NJQ, NN.

Society of Old Brooklynites. A Christmas reminder, being the names of about 8,000 persons confined on board the British prison ships (during the war of the American Revolution). 1888.   [702
NBLiHi, NJQ.

South Side Signal. Births, marriages and deaths from the *South Side Signal.* (Mounted clippings.)   [703
A complete file of this entire newspaper, published at Babylon, New York, is on deposit in the Babylon Public Library.
NBLiHi, NEh.

Southampton Colony Chapter, Daughters of the American Revolution. Tombstone inscriptions in Southampton and East Hampton towns (outside East Hampton village). 1939. [704
NEh.

Southampton, New York. Southampton local census, 1821. (MS.) [705
NBLiHi.

———— Southampton Presbyterian Church cemetery inscriptions. (MS.) [706
NNNGB.

Southampton, New York: Committee of the Town. Records of the Town of Southampton. 1639-1925. 8 vols. [707
Vols. 2 and 4 contain vital records.
DLC, DNDAR, MBNEH, MWA, N, NB, NBLiHi, NEh, NJQ, NN, NNNGB, NRvS, NSmB.

Southold, New York. Southold local papers, 1685-1765. (1 folder.) [708
NHi.

Sparrow, George. Tombstone inscriptions in the burial ground of the Old Bushwick Church. 1880. In *Kings County Genealogical Club Collections, 1,* No. 4, p. 45. [709
DLC, DNDAR, MBNEH, NBLiHi, NEh, NJQ, NN, NNNGB, USIGS.

Springer, Semon H. East of Nieuw Amsterdam; profiles: Queens people, past and present. In *Queens County Times,* 1946-1947. (Mounted clippings.) .[710
NN.

Star Directories. Star Directory of Long Island City, 1894-95. [711
NJQ.

Stiles, Henry R. A history of the city of Brooklyn. 1867-70. 3 vols. [712
CU, DLC, DNDAR, MBNEH, MdBP, MH, MiU, MiU-C, MWA, N, NB, NBB, NBC, NBG, NBLiHi, NEh, Nh, NIC, NjN, NjNbT, NjP, NJQ, NN, NNC, NNNGB, NSmB, OCl, OO, PSt, USIGS.

———— Illustrated history of Kings County, New York, 1683-1884. 1884. 2 vols. [713
DLC, MB, MdBP, MH, MWA, N, NB, NBB, NBC, NBLiHi, NEh, Nh, NIC, NJQ, NN, NNC, NNNGB, OClWHi.

———— Tombstone inscriptions from the Presbyterian churchyard of Southold. In *New York Geneal. and Biog. Record, 2:* 29-30. [714
Az, C, CaOTP, CL, CoD, CSf, Ct, CtHi, CtY, DLC, DNDAR, IaHi, IC, ICN, ICU, In, MB, MBAt, MBNEH, MdBP, MeHi, MH, MHi, Mi, MiD-B, MNF, MnHi, MnM, MoK, MoS, MWA, N, NB, NBLiHi, NBu, NBuG, Nc, NEh, Nh, NHC, NHi, NIC, NjNbS, NjPla, NJQ, NN, NNC, NNNGB, NR, OC, OCHP, OCl, OClWHi, OHi, PEa, PEr, PHi, PPi, PPL, USIGS, Wa, WaS, WM.

Stillwell, John Edwin. Record of the Court of Sessions of the West Riding of Yorkshire, 1676. In *Historical and Genealogical Miscellany,* 1903, vol. 1, pp. 224-239. [715
DLC, DNDAR, ICN, MBNEH, NBLiHi, NJQ, NN, NNNGB, OClWHi, USIGS.

Stillwell, William Henry. History of Gravesend.   [716
NBLiHi (MS. and typed copy) ; NEh (typed copy).

——————— Minutes of the Reformed Dutch Church of Brooklyn, 1660-1696.
1880.   (Typed.)   [717
NBLiHi.

——————— History of the Reformed Protestant Dutch Church of Gravesend.   Baptisms 1714-1890, marriages 1832-1890, deaths 1714-1891,
communicants 1763-1890 and officers, 1766-1806. 1892.   [718
DLC, MBNEH, N, NBLiHi, NEh, NJQ, NN, NNNGB, NSmB.

——————— History of the Reformed Dutch Church on Long Island. 1893.
(Typed.)   [719
NBLiHi.

Stony Brook, New York. Smith family burying ground, Main street,
Stony Brook. (Typed.)   [720
NBLiHi, NNNGB.

Stoothoff family. The Stoothoff papers. Dutch MS, and English trans-
lation by Frank L. Van Cleef.   [721
Some items printed in *Long Island Hist. Soc. Quarterly, 2*, pp. 76-80.
NBLiHi.

Stoutenburgh, Henry A(ugustus). A documentary history of het Ned-
erduytsche Gemeente, Dutch congregation of Oyster Bay, Queens
County, Island of Nassau, now Long Island. 1902-1907.   [722
Contains church records and also Luyster cemetery inscriptions, North Beach, New
York (vol. 2, p. 307).
DLC, MB, MBNEH, MWA, N, NBLiHi, NEh, NHu, NHuHi, NJQ, NN, NNNGB,
NRvS, NSmB, OClWHi, OO, PPPrHi, USlGS.

Street, Charles R(ufus). Huntington town records including Babylon,
Long Island, New York, 1653-1873. 1887+. 3 vols.   [723
This series is incomplete for the time it records.
DLC, DNDAR, MB, MBNEH, MdBP, MWA, N, NBLiHi, NEh, NHu, NHuHi, NJQ,
NN, NNC, NNNGB, NRvS, NSmB, USlGS.

Strong, Robert G(rier). A History of the town of Flatbush, New York.
1884.   [724
MWA, NBLiHi, NN.

Strong, Thomas M(orris). The History of the town of Flatbush, in Kings
County, Long Island. 1842.   [725
DLC, MBNEH, MWA, N, NB, NBC, NBLiHi, NEh, NjNbR, NjNbS, NJQ, NN,
NNNGB, NSmB, PHi, USlGS.

——————— The history of the town of Flatbush in Kings County. Second
edition, 1908.   [726
DLC, N, NBC, NJQ, NN, NNC.

Stryker-Rodda, Harriet. Records of the First Presbyterian Church of
Brooklyn, New York. Members, 1822-1897; marriages, baptisms and
deaths, 1877-1897. (Typed.)   [727
NBLiHi, NNNGB.

———— Flatlands Reformed Dutch Church consistory book, 1833-1835. Includes members contributing to pew and salary. (Typed.)   [728
NBLiHi.

———— Gravesend and New Utrecht deaths and transportations, 1870-1890, from the records of A. E. Stillwell, funeral director. (Typed.)
[729
NBLiHi.

———— Excerpts from the minutes of the Methodist Episcopal Church quarterly conferences of Kings County, 1844-1855. (Typed.)   [730
NBLiHi.

———— Vital records (and other genealogical data) from *The Long Island Democrat.* 1861-1880. (2 scrapbooks, indexed.)   [731
NBLiHi.

———— New Utrecht, New York. Grace Methodist Episcopal church-yard, 1832-1901; removals, 1901. From the original note book of Philip Pflaum. (Typed.)   [732
NBLiHi.

———— Fisherman's Methodist Church of Unionville, New York. Baptisms 1846-1890, marriages 1855-1885. (Typed.)   [733
NBLiHi.

Stryker-Rodda, Harriet and Kenn. Records of the Sixth Methodist Episcopal Church of Brooklyn (Eighteenth Street Church). Baptisms, 1856-1888, marriages 1856-1892, probationers and members 1856-1893. (Typed.)   [734
NBLiHi.

———— Records of the Reformed Dutch Church of Flatlands, 1737-1914. 3 vols. (Typed.)   [735
NBLiHi.

Stryker-Rodda, Kenn. Bay Ridge Methodist Church records. Baptisms, 1845-1902; marriages 1855-1901; members 1855-1901, and deaths and removals. 1953. (Typed.)   [736
NBLiHi.

———— Records of the Sixth Avenue Methodist Episcopal Church of Brooklyn, New York, 1884-1905. Baptisms, marriages, probationers, members, deaths and removals. (Typed.)   [737
NBLiHi.

———— Records of the Sabbath School of the Methodist Episcopal Church of New Utrecht (later, Bay Ridge and Grace Methodist Episcopal Churches). 1833-1845. 1953. (Typed.)   [738
NBLiHi.

Suffolk County, New York. Bicentennial history of Suffolk County (New York). 1885.   [739
CSmH, MH, MWA, NBLiHi, NNNGB.

———— Abstracts of wills, Suffolk County, subsequent to 1787, on file in the office of the Surrogate, at Riverhead.   [740
DNDAR, MBNEH, NBLiHi, NEh, NJQ, USlGS.

———— Index of deeds, Suffolk County, 1750-1837.   [741
NNNGB.

———— Suffolk County local papers, 1701-1814. (1 folder.)   [742
NHi.

———— Suffolk County Methodist Episcopal Churches. Steward's account book, 1795-1830. (MS.)   [743
NN (Manuscript Room).

Sullivan, Leonard. Inscriptions from the Powell cemetery at Bethpage. 1944. (Typed.)   [744
NNNGB.

———— Inscriptions from the Powell family cemetery at Central Park, New York. (Typed.)   [745
NBLiHi.

Swartwout, Henry. Henry Swartwout's deposition concerning 38 loyalists (of Kings County, New York). (MS.)   [746
NN.

Terry, Stewart T. Salmon records with ancestral and other notes. (Original MS and typescript of first 60 pages.)   [747
NBLiHi.

Thomas, Milton Halsey and Charles Shepard II. Index to the wills, administrations and guardianships of Kings County, 1650 to 1850. 1926.   [748
DLC, DNDAR, MBNEH, MiU-C, MWA, N, NBLiHi, NJQ, NN, NNNGB, OClWHi, PHi, USlGS.

Thompson, Benjamin. History of Long Island. First edition, 1839; second edition, 1844; third edition, revised and enlarged by Charles J. Werner, 3 vols., 1918.   [749
All three editions: DLC, DNDAR, N, NBLiHi, NJQ, NN. First edition only: AU, CSmH, CU, DSI-M, MB, MiU, NB, NNG, MWA, PP, PPG, PU; first and second editions: MBNEH, MWA, NEh, NHu, NHuHi, NIC, NjP, NSmB, OClWHi, PHi, PPL, USlGS, ViU; second edition only: IC, NjN, NNC, NNHi, OCl; first and third editions: NBB; second and third editions: NNNGB; third edition only: NBG, NRvS.

Thompson, Noyes L. History of Plymouth Church, Brooklyn, New York, with an alphabetical list of all persons who have ever been members of Plymouth Church; with admissions, deaths and dismissals: 1847-1872. 1873.   [750
MBNEH, NBLiHi, NN.

Thompson, Samuel. Diary of Dr. Samuel Thompson, 1800-1810 (including births, illnesses, deaths) and Thompson family papers, 1710-1858. (Setauket, New York.) (MS.)   [751
NN (Manuscript Room).

Thorpe, Isabel. Port Washington tombstone inscriptions. In *Early Settlers of New York State:* Flower Hill burial ground, *6*, p. 554; Monfort's farm burial ground, *6*, p. 570; *7*, p. 10; Old farm cemetery, *6*, p. 554; and the Old Mitchell burying ground, *6*, p. 570.   [752
DLC, NBLiHi, NN.

Todd, T. H. The Star directory of Long Island City, embracing a general directory of the residents of Hunter's Point, Blissville, Dutch Kills, Ravenswood, Astoria, Steinway and the German settlement and North Beach; also a classified business directory of the entire city.   [753
DLC, vol. 2, 1888-89; MWA, vol. 3, 1894-95; NB, vol. 2, 1888-89; NJQ, vol. 3, 1894-95.

Toedteberg, Emma. Inscriptions from the tombstones in the cemeteries of Farmingdale and Bethpage. 1894. (MS.)   [754
BETHPAGE: (Unnamed cemetery.)
FARMINGDALE: Yard near the Water Witch Engine House; a lot on the turnpike to Hempstead (Schnaderbeck).
NBLiHi.

Topographical Bureau of the Borough of Queens, New York. Historical collections of the Borough of Queens, copied from original reports in the Topographical Bureau. 15 vols. (Typed.)   [755
NJQ.

Trow's Directories. (See also Polk.) Trow business directory of the borough of Queens, city of New York, also residential directories of Flushing, Jamaica, Long Island City and Richmond Hill, vols. 1 to 10, 1898-1912. Also: Trow's business directory and residential directory of the borough of Queens, city of New York, and residential directory of Flushing, Jamaica, Long Island City and Richmond Hill.   [756
DLC, vols. 1-10; NB, vol. 5, 1902; NN, vol. 9, 1909/10; vol. 10, 1912; NJQ, vol. 1-2, 1898-99; vol. 4, 1901; vols. 6-10, 1904-1912.

Trumbull, J(ames) Hammond. Colonial records of Connecticut, 1636-1665.   [757
Contains records of many Long Island inhabitants.
NBLiHi, NN, NNNGB.

Underhill, David Harris and Francis Jay Underhill. Locust Valley, New York: the Underhill burying ground. 1926.   [758
DLC, MBNEH, N, NB, NBLiHi, NEh, NJQ, USIGS.

United States Government: Department of Commerce; Bureau of the Census. Heads of families at the First Census of the United States, taken in the year 1790. New York State. 1908.   [759
DLC, DNDAR, DNGS, IaU, MB, MBAt, MBNEH, MH, MiU-C, MnU, MWA, MWiW-C, NBLiHi. NEh, NN, NNNGB, NNS, RHi, RPJCB, ScC, USIGS, ViU.

United States Government: Department of Commerce; Bureau of the Census. Federal Census, 1800. Published by towns in *New York Geneal. and Biog. Record.*   [760

BROOKHAVEN: *56*, pp. 227-280, 323-329.
BROOKLYN: *55*, pp. 124-129.
BUSHWICK: *55*, pp. 129-130.
EAST HAMPTON: *56*, pp. 272-276.
FLATBUSH: *55*, pp. 23-24.
FLATLANDS (NEW AMERSFOORT): *55*, p. 25.
FLUSHING: *54*, pp. 213-218.
GRAVESEND: *55*, pp. 121-122.
HUNTINGTON: *55*, pp. 339-348; *56*, pp. 9-10.
ISLIP: *56*, pp. 14-16.
JAMAICA: *54*, pp. 120-121; 210-213.
NEWTOWN: *54*, pp. 218-219, 346-349.
NEW UTRECHT: *55*, pp. 122-123.
NORTH HEMPSTEAD: *54*, pp. 20-26.
OYSTER BAY: *54*, pp. 350-355; *55*, pp. 16-22.
RIVERHEAD: *56*, pp. 330-332; *57*, pp. 55-56.
SHELTER ISLAND: *56*, pp. 271-272.
SMITHTOWN: *56*, pp. 10-14.
SOUTH HEMPSTEAD (HEMPSTEAD): *54*, pp. 26-29, 112-120.
SOUTHAMPTON: *56*, pp. 127-137.
SOUTHOLD: *57*, pp. 56-62.
Az, C, CaOTP, CL, CoD, CSf, Ct, CtHi, CtY, DLC, DNDAR, IaHi, IC, ICN, ICU, In, MB, MBAt, MBNEH, MdBP, MeHi, MH, MHi, Mi, MiD-B, MNF, MnHi, MnM, MoK, MoS, MWA, N, NB, NBLiHi, NBu, NBuG, Nc, NEh, Nh, NHC, NHi, NIC, NjNbS, NjPla, NJQ, NN, NNC, NNNGB, NR, OC, OCHP, OCl, OClWHi, OHi, PEa, PEr, PHi, PPi, PPL, USlGS, Wa, WaS, WM.

———— Census population schedules (all of Long Island), 1800-1880. Microfilm.   [761
DNA, NBLiHi, NJQ (also 1850 in typescript), NNNGB (1830).

———— Census of Kings County, 1850, 1860, 1870, 1880.   [762
MS transcript in the KING'S COUNTY CLERK'S OFFICE, BROOKLYN.

———— Census of Suffolk County, 1860.   [763
MS transcript in the SUFFOLK COUNTY CLERK'S OFFICE, RIVERHEAD.

———— Census of Veterans and Widows, 1890.   [763a
DNA, NBLiHi, NJQ.

United States: Department of the Interior, Pension Office. List of pensioners on the rolls January 1, 1883. 5 vols.   [764
NBLiHi, NN, NNNGB.

United States Provost Marshal, First Congressional District. Queens County enrollment list, 1863.   [765
NBLiHi, NJQ.

United States Provost Marshal, Second Congressional District. List of persons enrolled in the seventeenth ward, Brooklyn, 1863. Also, report of the Treasurer on amounts received from drafted men, 1865.   [766
NJQ.

United States Provost Marshal's Office. Lists of persons enrolled in Brooklyn, Gravesend, New Utrecht, New Lotts, Flatbush and Flatlands, 1863. Original pamphlets, bound by towns, and microfilm.   [767
NBLiHi.

United States — State Department. A census of pensioners for revolutionary or military service . . . under the Act for . . . the sixth census. 1841. **[768**
NBLiHi, NN, NNNGB.

United States — War Department. Letter from the Secretary of War transmitting a report . . . of every person placed on the pension list in pursuance of the Act of the 18th of March, 1818. 1820. **[769**
NBLiHi, NN, NNNGB.

———— Report from the Secretary of War . . . in relation to the pension establishment of the United States. 1835. vol. 2: The Middle States.
NBLiHi, NN, NNNGB. **[770**

United States Works Progress Administration: The Historical Records Survey. Inventory of county and borough archives of New York City. No. 2: Kings County. **[771**
NBLiHi, NN.

———— Guide to the Public Vital Statistics, Records of New York State. Locations where births, marriages and deaths are filed. 3 vols. (Mimeographed.) **[772**

AMITYVILLE, town of Babylon, Suffolk county
Births from 1894: Village clerk, Amityville.
Marriages from 1894: Town clerk, Babylon.
Deaths, 1894-1929: Village clerk, Amityville.

ASHAROKEN, town of Huntington, Suffolk county
Births from 1881: Town clerk, Huntington.
Marriages from 1925: Town clerk, Huntington.
Deaths, 1847-1863: Registrar of vital statistics, Huntington.
Deaths from 1881: Town clerk, Huntington.

BABYLON, town of, Suffolk county
Births from 1881 }
Marriages from 1881 } Town clerk, Babylon.
Deaths from 1881 }

BABYLON (village), town of Babylon, Suffolk county
Births from 1894 }
Marriages from 1893 } Town clerk, Babylon.
Deaths from 1894 }

BAXTER ESTATES, town of North Hempstead, Nassau county
Births from 1931 }
Marriages from 1931 } Town clerk, Manhasset.
Deaths from 1931 }

BAYVILLE, town of Oyster Bay, Nassau county
Births from 1919 }
Marriages from 1919 } Town clerk, Oyster Bay.
Deaths from 1919 }

BELLEROSE, town of Hempstead, Nassau county
Births from 1925: Registrar of vital statistics, Bellerose.
Marriages from 1924: Town clerk, Hempstead.
Deaths from 1925: Registrar of vital statistics, Bellerose.

BELLE TERRE, town of Brookhaven, Suffolk county
Births from 1932 }
Marriages from 1931 } Town clerk, Patchogue.
Deaths from 1932 }

BELLPORT, town of Brookhaven, Suffolk county
Births from 1910   ⎫
Marriages from 1910   ⎬   Village clerk, Bellport.
Deaths from 1910   ⎭

BRIGHTWATERS, town of Islip, Suffolk county
Births from 1917: Village clerk, Brightwaters.
Marriages from 1916: Town clerk, Islip.
Deaths from 1917: Village clerk, Brightwaters.

BROOKHAVEN (village), town of Brookhaven, Suffolk county
Births from 1881   ⎫
Marriages from 1881   ⎬   Town clerk, Patchogue.
Deaths from 1881   ⎭

BROOKLYN (city and borough), Kings county
Births from 1866   ⎫   Dept. of Health, Municipal bldg., Brooklyn,
Marriages from 1866   ⎬
Deaths from 1862   ⎭   and City clerk's office, the same.

BROOKVILLE, town of Oyster Bay, Nassau county
Births from 1932   ⎫
Marriages from 1931   ⎬   Town clerk, Oyster Bay.
Deaths from 1932   ⎭

CEDARHURST, town of Hempstead, Nassau county
Births from 1911: Village clerk, Cedarhurst.
Marriages from 1910: Town clerk, Hempstead.
Deaths from 1911: Village clerk, Cedarhurst.

CENTRE ISLAND, town of Oyster Bay, Nassau county
Births from 1926   ⎫
Marriages from 1926   ⎬   Town clerk, Oyster Bay.
Deaths from 1926   ⎭

COLLEGE POINT, town of Flushing, Queens county
Births, 1889-1898   ⎫
Marriages, 1871-1898 ⎬   Dept. of Health, Jamaica.
Deaths, 1881-1898   ⎭

COW NECK, town of Oyster Bay, Nassau county
Births from 1929   ⎫
Marriages from 1927   ⎬   Town clerk, Oyster Bay.
Deaths from 1929   ⎭

DERING HARBOR, town of Shelter Island, Suffolk county
Births from 1927: Village clerk, Shelter Island.
Marriages from 1916: Town clerk, Shelter Island.
Deaths from 1927: Village clerk, Shelter Island.

EAST HAMPTON, town of, Suffolk county
Births from 1881   ⎫
Marriages from 1881   ⎬   Town clerk, East Hampton.
Deaths from 1881   ⎭

EAST HAMPTON (village), town of East Hampton, Suffolk county
Births from 1921: Registrar of vital statistics, East Hampton.
Marriages from 1920: Town clerk, East Hampton.
Deaths from 1921: Registrar of vital statistics, East Hampton.

EAST HILLS, town of North Hempstead, Nassau county
Births from 1932: Town clerk, Manhasset.
Marriages from 1931: Town clerk, Manhasset.
Deaths from 1937: Village clerk, Roslyn.

EAST ROCKAWAY, town of Hempstead, Nassau county
Births from 1900   ⎫   Village clerk, East Rockaway, and, in part,
Marriages from 1900   ⎬
Deaths from 1900   ⎭   Town clerk, Hempstead.

LAST WILLISTON, town of North Hempstead, Nassau county
Births from 1926: Village clerk, East Williston.
Marriages from 1926: Town clerk, Manhasset.
Deaths from 1926: Village clerk, East Williston.

FARMINGDALE, town of Oyster Bay, Nassau county
Births from 1904 ⎫ In part in three places: Village clerk,
Marriages, 1904-1912; 1912-1914 ⎬ Farmingdale; Registrar of vital statistics,
Deaths from 1904 ⎭ Farmingdale; and Town clerk, Oyster Bay.

FAR ROCKAWAY, town of Jamaica, Queens county
Births, 1889-1897 ⎫ Dept. of Health, Jamaica.
Deaths, 1881-1898 ⎭

(Far Rockaway was originally in the town of Hempstead)

FLATBUSH, town of, Kings county
Births, 1847-1851 ⎫ Dept. of Health, Municipal bldg.,
Marriages, 1847-1851; 1880-1894 ⎬ Brooklyn.
Deaths, 1847-1851; 1880-1894 ⎭

FLATLANDS, town of, Kings county
Births, 1880-1895 ⎫ Dept. of Health, Municipal bldg.,
Marriages, 1880-1895 ⎬ Brooklyn.
Deaths, 1880-1894 ⎭

FLORAL PARK, town of Hempstead, Nassau county
Births from 1908: Village clerk, Floral Park.
Marriages from 1908: Town clerk, Hempstead.
Deaths from 1908: Village clerk, Floral Park.

FLOWER HILL, town of North Hempstead, Nassau county
Births from 1931 ⎫
Marriages from 1931 ⎬ Town clerk, Manhasset.
Deaths from 1931 ⎭

FLUSHING, town of, Queens county
Births, 1881-1897 ⎫
Marriages, 1871-1898 ⎬ Dept. of Health, Jamaica.
Deaths, 1847-1848; 1856-1873 ⎭

FLUSHING (village), town of Flushing, Queens county
Births, 1889-1897 ⎫
Marriages, 1871-1898 ⎬ Dept. of Health, Jamaica.
Deaths, 1881-1898 ⎭

FREEPORT, town of Hempstead, Nassau county
Births from 1894 ⎫
Marriages, 1894-1908 ⎬ Village clerk, Freeport.
Deaths, 1894-1908 ⎭

GARDEN CITY, town of Hempstead, Nassau county
Births from 1919: Village clerk, Garden City.
Marriages from 1919: Town clerk, Hempstead.
Deaths from 1920: Village clerk, Garden City.

GLEN COVE, town of Oyster Bay, Nassau county
Births from 1918: Registrar of Vital Statistics, Glen Cove.
Marriages from 1918: Registrar of Vital Statistics, Glen Cove.
Deaths from 1918: Registrar of Vital Statistics, Glen Cove.

GRAVESEND, town of, Kings county
Births, 1880-1894 ⎫
Marriages, 1880-1894 ⎬ Dept. of Health, Municipal bldg., Brooklyn.
Deaths, 1880-1894 ⎭

GREAT NECK, town of North Hempstead, Nassau county
Births from 1925 ⎫
Marriages from 1921 ⎬ Town clerk, Manhasset.
Deaths from 1925 ⎭

GREAT NECK ESTATES, town of North Hempstead, Nassau county
Births from 1925: Village clerk, Great Neck.

Marriages from 1911 ⎫
Deaths from 1925 ⎭ Town clerk, Manhasset.

GREAT NECK PLAZA, town of North Hempstead, Nassau county
Births from 1930 ⎫
Marriages from 1930 ⎬ Town clerk, Manhasset.
Deaths from 1930 ⎭

GREENPORT, town of Southold, Suffolk county
Births from 1881 ⎫
Marriages, 1881-1907* ⎬ Village clerk, Greenport.
Deaths from 1881 ⎭
*Marriages of later date filed with the Town clerk, Southold.

HEAD OF THE HARBOR, town of Smithtown, Suffolk county
Births, 1848-1849; from 1881 ⎫
Marriages, 1848-1849; from 1928 ⎬ Town clerk, Kings Park.
Deaths, 1848-1849; 1929-1934; others from 1881 ⎭

HEMPSTEAD, town of, Nassau county
Births from 1889: Registrar of vital statistics, Hempstead.
Marriages, 1889-1901: Registrar of vital statistics, Hempstead; after 1908, for
    North Hempstead: Town clerk, Manhasset.
Deaths, 1889-1901: Registrar of vital statistics, Hempstead.

HEMPSTEAD (village), town of Hempstead, Nassau county
Births, 1847-1849; from 1881 ⎫
Marriages, 1847-1849; from 1881 ⎬ Town clerk, Hempstead.
Deaths, 1847-1849; from 1881 ⎭

HEWLETT BAY PARK, town of Hempstead, Nassau county
Births from 1930: Village clerk, Hewlett Bay Park.
Marriages from 1928: Town clerk, Hempstead.
Deaths from 1930: Village clerk, Hewlett Bay Park.

HEWLETT HARBOR, town of Hempstead, Nassau county
Births from 1931 ⎫
Marriages from 1925 ⎬ Town clerk, Hempstead.
Deaths from 1931 ⎭

HEWLETT NECK, town of Hempstead, Nassau county
Births from 1936 ⎫
Marriages from 1927 ⎬ Town clerk, Hempstead.
Deaths from 1936 ⎭

HUNTINGTON, town of, Suffolk county
Births, 1847-1867; from 1881 ⎫
Marriages, 1847-1867; from 1881 ⎬ Town clerk, Huntington.
Deaths, 1847-1867; from 1881 ⎭

HUNTINGTON BAY, town of Huntington, Suffolk county
Births from 1924 ⎫
Marriages from 1924 ⎬ Town clerk, Huntington.
Deaths from 1924 ⎭

ISLAND PARK, town of Hempstead, Nassau county
Births from 1927 ⎫
Marriages from 1927 ⎬ Village clerk, Island Park.
Deaths from 1927 ⎭

ISLIP, town of, Suffolk county
Births from 1881 ⎫
Marriages from 1881 ⎬ Town clerk, Islip.
Deaths from 1881 ⎭

JAMAICA, town of, Queens county
Births, 1881-1898
Marriages, 1847-1849; 1856-1898 } Dept. of Health, Jamaica.*
Deaths, 1881-1898
*to New York city after January 1, 1898.

JAMAICA (village), town of Jamaica, Queens county
Births, 1889-1898
Marriages, 1871-1898 } Dept. of Health, Jamaica.

KENSINGTON, town of North Hempstead, Nassau county
Births from 1925
Marriages from 1921 } Town clerk, Manhasset.
Deaths from 1925

KINGS COUNTY
Marriages from 1908: County clerk, Brooklyn.

KINGS POINT, town of North Hempstead, Nassau county
Births from 1925: Village clerk, Kings Point.
Marriages from 1924: Town clerk, Manhasset.
Deaths from 1925: Town clerk, Manhasset.

LAKE SUCCESS, town of North Hempstead, Nassau county
Births from 1929
Marriages from 1927 } Town clerk, Manhasset.
Deaths from 1929

LATTINGTOWN, town of Oyster Bay, Nassau county
Births from 1933
Marriages from 1931 } Town clerk, Oyster Bay.
Deaths from 1933

LAURELTON, town of Oyster Bay, Nassau county
Births from 1926
Marriages from 1926 } Town clerk, Oyster Bay.
Deaths from 1926

LAWRENCE, town of Hempstead, Nassau county
Births, 1923-1931
Marriages, 1901-1902 } Village clerk, Lawrence.
Deaths, 1901-1937

LINDENHURST, town of Babylon, Suffolk county
Births from 1928: Village clerk, Lindenhurst.
Marriages from 1927: Town clerk, Babylon.
Deaths from 1928: Village clerk, Lindenhurst.

LLOYDS HARBOR, town of Huntington, Suffolk county
Births from 1927
Marriages from 1926 } Town clerk, Huntington.
Deaths from 1927

LONG BEACH, town of Hempstead, Nassau county
Births, from 1922
Marriages, from 1913 } City clerk, Long Beach.
Deaths, from 1913

LONG ISLAND CITY, town of Newtown, Queens county
Births, 1881-1892
Marriages, 1871-1898 } Dept. of Health, Jamaica.
Deaths, 1871-1897

LYNBROOK, town of Hempstead, Nassau county
Births, from 1911: Village clerk, Lynbrook.
Marriages, from 1911: Town clerk, Hempstead.
Deaths from 1911: Village clerk, Lynbrook.

MALVERNE, town of Hempstead, Nassau county
Births from 1921   ⎫
Marriages from 1921   ⎬   Register of vital statistics, Malverne.
Deaths from 1921   ⎭

MANORHAVEN, town of North Hempstead, Nassau county
Births from 1934   ⎫
Marriages from 1930   ⎬   Village clerk, Manorhaven.
Deaths from 1934   ⎭

MASSAPEQUA PARK, town of Oyster Bay, Nassau county
Births, from 1931   ⎫
Marriages, from 1931   ⎬   Town clerk, Oyster Bay.
Deaths, from 1931   ⎭

MATINECOCK, town of Oyster Bay, Nassau county
Births, from 1928   ⎫
Marriages, from 1928   ⎬   Town clerk, Oyster Bay.
Deaths, from 1928   ⎭

MILL NECK, town of Oyster Bay, Nassau county
Births, from 1927   ⎫
Marriages, from 1925   ⎬   Town clerk, Oyster Bay.
Deaths, from 1927   ⎭

MINEOLA, town of North Hempstead, Nassau county
Births, from 1907: Village clerk, Mineola.
Marriages, from 1906: Town clerk, Manhasset.
Deaths, from 1907: Village clerk, Mineola.

MUNSEY PARK, town of North Hempstead, Nassau county
Births, from 1931   ⎫
Marriages, from 1930   ⎬   Town clerk, Manhasset.
Deaths, from 1931   ⎭

MUTTONTOWN, town of Oyster Bay, Nassau county
Births, from 1932   ⎫
Marriages, from 1931   ⎬   Town clerk, Oyster Bay.
Deaths, from 1932   ⎭

NASSAU COUNTY
Marriages, from 1908: County clerk, Mineola.

NEW HYDE PARK, town of North Hempstead, Nassau county
Births, from 1927: Village clerk, New Hyde Park.
Marriages, from 1927: Town clerk, Manhasset.
Deaths, from 1927: Village clerk, New Hyde Park.

NEW LOTS, town of, Kings county
Births, 1881-1886   ⎫
Marriages, 1881-1886   ⎬   Dept. of Health, Brooklyn.
Deaths, 1881-1886   ⎭

NEWTOWN, town of, Queens county
Births, 1847-1849; 1881-1898   ⎫
Deaths, 1888-1898   ⎬   Dept. of Health, Jamaica.

NEW UTRECHT, town of, Kings county
Births, 1880-1894   ⎫
Marriages, 1880-1894   ⎬   Dept. of Health, Brooklyn.
Deaths, 1880-1894   ⎭

NISSEQUOGUE, town of Smithtown, Suffolk county
Births, 1931-1934   ⎫
Marriages, from 1926   ⎬   Town clerk, Kings Park.
Deaths, 1931-1934   ⎭

NORTH HAVEN, town of Southampton, Suffolk county
  Births, from 1931: Village clerk, Sag Harbor.
  Marriages, from 1931: Town clerk, Southampton.
  Deaths, from 1931: Village clerk, Sag Harbor.

NORTH HEMPSTEAD, town of, Nassau county
  Births, 1847-1849 and from 1881
  Marriages, 1847-1849, 1881-1898 and from 1928 } Town clerk, Manhasset.
  Deaths, 1847-1849, 1881-1899 and from 1928

NORTH HILLS, town of North Hempstead, Nassau county
  Births, from 1930
  Marriages, from 1929 } Town clerk, Manhasset.
  Deaths, from 1930

NORTHPORT, town of Huntington, Suffolk county
  Births, from 1894: Village clerk, Northport.
  Marriages, 1894-1907: Village clerk, Northport.
  Marriages, from 1907: Town clerk, Huntington.
  Deaths, from 1894: Village clerk, Northport.

NORTHVILLE, town of Riverhead, Suffolk county
  Births, 1927-1930
  Marriages, 1921-1930 } Town clerk, Riverhead.
  Deaths, 1927-1930
  The village was dissolved in 1930.

OCEAN BEACH, town of Islip, Suffolk county
  Births, from 1881
  Marriages, from 1921 } Town clerk, Islip.
  Deaths, from 1881

OLD BROOKVILLE, town of Oyster Bay, Nassau county
  Births, from 1930
  Marriages, from 1929 } Town clerk, Oyster Bay.
  Deaths, from 1930

OLD FIELD, town of Brookhaven, Suffolk county
  Births, from 1929: Village clerk, Old Field.
  Marriages, from 1927: Town clerk, Patchogue.
  Deaths, from 1929: Village clerk, Old Field.

OLD WESTBURY, town of North Hempstead, Nassau county
  Births, from 1924
  Marriages, from 1924 } Town clerk, Manhasset.
  Deaths, from 1924

OYSTER BAY, town of, Nassau county
  Births, 1847-1850 and from 1881
  Marriages, 1847-1850 and from 1881 } Town clerk, Oyster Bay.
  Deaths, 1847-1850 and from 1881

OYSTER BAY COVE, town of Oyster Bay, Nassau county
  Births, from 1924
  Marriages, from 1931 } Town clerk, Oyster Bay.
  Deaths, from 1924

PATCHOGUE, town of Brookhaven, Suffolk county
  Births, from 1893: Village clerk, Patchogue.
  Marriages, 1894-1912: Village clerk, Patchogue.
  Marriages, from 1912: Town clerk, Patchogue.
  Deaths, from 1893: Village clerk, Patchogue.

PEQUOTT, town of Brookhaven, Suffolk county
  Births, from 1935: Village clerk, East Setauket.
  Marriages, from 1931: Town clerk, Patchogue.
  Deaths, from 1936: Village clerk, East Setauket.

PLANDOME, town of North Hempstead, Nassau county
Births from 1911
Marriages, from 1911   } Town clerk, Manhasset.
Deaths, from 1911

PLANDOME HEIGHTS, town of North Hempstead, Nassau county
Births, from 1930
Marriages, from 1929   } Town clerk, Manhasset.
Deaths, from 1930

PLANDOME MANOR, town of North Hempstead, Nassau county
Births, from 1932
Marriages, from 1931   } Town clerk, Manhasset.
Deaths, from 1932

PORT WASHINGTON NORTH, town of North Hempstead, Nassau county
Births, from 1934: Registrar of vital statistics, Manhasset.
Marriages, from 1934: Town clerk, Manhasset.
Deaths, from 1934: Registrar of vital statistics, Manhasset.

QUEENS BOROUGH
Births, from 1898: Dept. of Health, Jamaica.
Marriages, from 1908: County clerk, Jamaica.

QUOGUE, town of Southampton, Suffolk county
Births, from 1929: Village clerk, Quogue.
Marriages, from 1928: Town clerk, Southampton.
Deaths, from 1929: Village clerk, Quogue.

RICHMOND HILL, town of Jamaica, Queens county
Births, 1895-1897
Marriages, 1871-1898   } Dept. of Health, Jamaica.
Deaths, 1881-1898

RIVERHEAD, town of, Suffolk county
Births, from 1881
Marriages, from 1881   } Town clerk, Riverhead.
Deaths, from 1881

ROCKAWAY, town of Hempstead, Nassau county
Births, 1897-1898
Marriages, 1871-1898   } Dept. of Health, Jamaica.
Deaths, 1881-1898

ROCKVILLE CENTRE, town of Hempstead, Nassau county
Births: 1893-1916; 1920-1933   } Village clerk,
Marriages: 1893-1907   Rockville
Deaths: 1898-1916; 1917-1919; 1920-1933; from 1934 } Centre.

ROSLYN, town of North Hempstead, Nassau county
Births, from 1932: Village clerk, Roslyn.
Marriages, from 1932: Town clerk, Manhasset.
Deaths, from 1932: Village clerk, Roslyn.

ROSLYN ESTATES, town of North Hempstead, Nassau county
Births, from 1932
Marriages, from 1931   } Town clerk, Manhasset.
Deaths, from 1932

RUSSELL GARDENS, town of North Hempstead, Nassau county
Births, from 1932
Marriages, from 1931   } Town clerk, Manhasset.
Deaths, from 1932

SADDLE ROCK, town of North Hempstead, Nassau county
Births, from 1932
Marriages, from 1911   } Town clerk, Manhasset.
Deaths, from 1932

SAG HARBOR, town of Southampton, Suffolk county
Births, from 1881: Village clerk, Sag Harbor.
Marriages, 1881-1908: Village clerk, Sag Harbor.
Marriages, from 1908: Town clerk, Southampton.
Deaths, from 1881: Village clerk, Sag Harbor.

SHELTER ISLAND, town of, Suffolk county
Births, from 1881 ⎫
Marriages, from 1917 ⎬ Town clerk, Islip.
Deaths, from 1881 ⎭

SANDS POINT, town of North Hempstead, Nassau county
Births, from 1921 ⎫
Marriages, from 1910 ⎬ Town clerk, Manhasset.
Deaths, from 1921 ⎭

SEA CLIFF, town of Oyster Bay, Nassau county
Births, from 1890: Village clerk, Sea Cliff.
Marriages, from 1890-1908: Village clerk, Sea Cliff.
Marriages, from 1908: Town clerk, Oyster Bay.
Deaths, from 1890: Village clerk, Sea Cliff.

SHELTER ISLAND, town of, Suffolk county
Births, from 1881 ⎫
Marriages, from 1881 ⎬ Town clerk, Shelter Island.
Deaths, from 1881 ⎭

SHOREHAM, town of Brookhaven, Suffolk county
Births, from 1927: Village clerk, Shoreham.
Marriages, from 1913: Town clerk, Patchogue.
Deaths, from 1927: Village clerk, Shoreham.

SMITHTOWN, town of, Suffolk county
Births, 1848-1849; from 1881 ⎫
Marriages, 1848-1849; from 1881 ⎬ Town clerk, Kings Park.
Deaths, 1848-1849; 1929-1934; from 1881 ⎭

SOUTH FLORAL PARK, town of Hempstead, Nassau county
Births, from 1926 Registrar of vital statistics, Floral Park.
Marriages, from 1925: Town clerk, Hempstead.
Deaths, from 1926: Registrar of vital statistics, Floral Park.

SOUTHAMPTON, town of, Suffolk county
Births, 1640-1880; from 1881 ⎫
Marriages, 1640-1880; from 1881 ⎬ Town clerk, Southampton.
Deaths, 1640-1800; from 1881 ⎭

SOUTHAMPTON (village), town of Southampton, Suffolk county
Births, from 1894: Village clerk, Southampton.
Marriages, from 1894: Town clerk, Southampton.
Deaths, from 1894: Village clerk, Southampton.

SOUTHOLD, town of, Suffolk county
Births, from 1881 ⎫
Marriages, from 1881 ⎬ Town clerk, Southold.
Deaths, from 1881 ⎭

STEWART MANOR, town of Hempstead, Nassau county
Births, from 1928: Village clerk, Stewart Manor.
Marriages, from 1927: Town clerk, Hempstead.
Deaths, from 1928: Village clerk, Stewart Manor.

SUFFOLK COUNTY
Births, 1847-1853 ⎫
Marriages, 1847-1853: 1908-1936 ⎬ County clerk, Riverhead.
Deaths, 1847-1853 ⎭

THOMASTON, town of North Hempstead, Nassau county
Births, from 1931 ⎫
Marriages, from 1931 ⎬ Town clerk, Manhasset.
Deaths, from 1931 ⎭

UPPER BROOKVILLE, town of Oyster Bay, Nassau county
Births, from 1933 ⎫
Marriages, from 1932 ⎬ Town clerk, Oyster Bay.
Deaths, from 1933 ⎭

VALLEY STREAM, town of Hempstead, Nassau county
Births, from 1925: Village clerk, Valley Stream.
Marriages, from 1925: Town clerk, Hempstead.
Deaths, 1925-1927; from 1939: Village clerk, Valley Stream.

VILLAGE OF THE BRANCH, town of Smithtown, Suffolk county
Births, from 1881 ⎫
Marriages, from 1927 ⎬ Town clerk, Kings Park.
Deaths, from 1881 ⎭

VILLAGE OF THE LANDING, town of Smithtown, Suffolk county
Births, from 1881 ⎫
Marriages, from 1927 ⎬ Town clerk, Kings Park.
Deaths, from 1881 ⎭

WESTBURY, town of North Hempstead, Nassau county
Births, from 1932 ⎫
Deaths, from 1932 ⎬ Town clerk, Manhasset.

WESTHAMPTON BEACH, town of Southampton, Suffolk county
Births, from 1928 ⎫
Marriages, from 1928 ⎬ Village clerk, Westhampton Beach.
Deaths, from 1928 ⎭

WHITESTONE, town of Flushing, Queens county
Deaths, 1881-1898: Dept. of Health, Jamaica.

WILLISTON PARK, town of North Hempstead, Nassau county
Births, from 1927: Village clerk, Williston Park.
Marriages, from 1926: Town clerk, Manhasset.
Deaths, from 1927: Village clerk, Williston Park.

WOODSBURGH, town of Hempstead, Nassau county
Deaths, from 1928: Registrar of vital statistics, Lawrence.

DLC, MBNEH, NBLiHi, NJQ, NN, NNNGB, OCl, OCU, OO, ViU.

———— History map of Flushing (and adjacent localities). Historical
and genealogical items. (Microfilm.)   [773
NNNGB.

———— Guide to vital statistics in the City of New York. Churches—
boroughs of Queens, Brooklyn, 2 vols. (Mimeographed.)   [773a
NBLiHi, NNNGB.

———— Minutes of the town courts of Newtown, Long Island, 1656-1690.
DLC, MBNEH, NBLiHi, NEh, NJQ, NN, NNNGB, ViU.   [774

———— Town minutes of Newtown, 1653-1734. 2 vols.   [775
DLC, MBNEH, NBLiHi, NEh, NJQ, NN, NNNGB, ViU.

United States Works Progress Administration. Register of baptisms,
marriages and deaths, South Bushwick Reformed Church, 1851-1901;
minutes 1851-1873, 1915-1917. 1937. (Typed.) WPA Project No.
165-97-6999 (6115).   [776
NBLiHi, NJQ, NNNGB.

Vail, Louis T(ooker). Complete tombstone inscriptions of Oakland cemetery, Sag Harbor, Long Island. [777
NEh.

———— Tombstone inscriptions from cemeteries in and near Sag Harbor. (Typed.) [778
Includes Old burying ground; Noyack cemetery; Rogers family cemetery; Havens cemetery at North Haven, 1950.
NBLiHi, NEh, NN, NNNGB.

———— Records of the Presbyterian church of Sag Harbor. Baptisms, 1797-1832; marriages, 1797-1835; and deaths, 1795-1833. (Typed.)
NBLiHi, NNNGB. [779

———— Miscellaneous vital records of Sag Harbor as copied from newspapers, 1817 to 1832, with a few earlier. (Typed.) [780
NNNGB.

———— Tombstone inscriptions in Oakland cemetery, Sag Harbor. (Typed.) [781
NBLiHi, NEh, NN.

Vallee, M. B. History of Flushing, New York. [782
NNNGB (microfilm).

Van Brunt, Adriance. Diary and journal, 1828-1830. (MS.) [783
NN (Manuscript Room).

Van Buren, DeWitt. Brooklyn marriage records from the *Herald* and the *Morning Herald,* 1836, 1838. 1935. (Typed.) [784
NBLiHi.

———— Manuscript records of the town of Bushwick, 1660-1825. 1935. (Typed.) [785
NBLiHi, NNNGB.

———— Flatbush town records. Liber A, 1670-1708, abstracted. (Typed.) [786
NBLiHi, NNNGB.

———— Abstracts of wills, Kings County, recorded in Brooklyn, 1787-1843. 1934. 7 vols. (Typed.) [787
MBNEH, NBLiHi, NNNGB.

———— Baptismal records from the register of the Southold Presbyterian Church, 1833-1891. (Typed.) [788
NBLiHi, NNNGB.

———— Membership records of the Southold Presbyterian Church, 1800-1892. (Typed.) [789
NBLiHi, NEh, NNNGB.

———— Land records of Suffolk County, New York. Liber A, 1687-1704. (Typed.) [790
NNNGB.

Van Buren, Elizabeth R. Brookhaven, New York, cemetery inscriptions. Union cemetery of the Presbyterian parish of Middle Town (Coram) ; Methodist cemetery of Middle Town; and a family burying ground on the Middle county road.   [791
MBNEH, NBLiHi, NEh, NNNGB.

———— Coram and Selden cemetery inscriptions. 1934. (Typed.) [792
CORAM: Old Baptist cemetery; Methodist Episcopal Church cemetery; O'Doherty family burial ground; Davis family burial ground.
SELDEN: Longbotham and Norton family burying grounds.
NBLiHi.

———— Union cemetery, Middle Town Road, Brookhaven. 1932. Inscriptions. (Typed.)   [793
NEh, NNNGB.

———— Tombstone inscriptions of Suffolk County. Family cemeteries: Wood, Buffett, Whitman, Carll and Nostrand families, located on Deer Park Avenue and upper Half Hollow Hills road, town of Huntington.
NBLiHi, NEh.   [794

———— Baiting Hollow cemetery in Riverhead, New York. Tombstone inscriptions. 1933. (Typed.)   [795
NBLiHi, NEh.

———— Abstracts of wills, Suffolk County, New York, 1787-1847. Libers A - H, in the office of the Surrogate at Riverhead, New York. 3 vols.
DNDAR, MBNEH, NBLiHi, NEh, NNNGB.   [796

———— Intestate records of Suffolk County, 1787-1829. (Libers A to E.) (Typed.)   [797
NBLiHi.

———— Tombstone inscriptions of . . . Yaphank: Hawkins, Homan-Owen and Homan family burying grounds; Presbyterian Church, St. Andrews Protestant Episcopal Church cemeteries; Yaphank Cemetery Association.   [798
NBLiHi, NNNGB.

Van Deyn, Cornelius. Record book of Garret Nostrant and Fernandus Sujdam as executors of Cornelius Van Deyn of Brooklyn, 1782-1787. (MS.)   [799
NHi.

Van Wyke, Frederick. Keskachauge, or the first white settlement on Long Island. 1924.   [800
DLC, MBNEH, N, NBLiHi, NEh, NHu, NJQ, NN, NNNGB, USIGS.

Vanderbilt, Gertrude Lefferts. The social history of Flatbush. 1881.
[801
CU, DLC, MdBP, MiU, MWA, N, NB, NBB, NBC, NBLiHi, NEh, NHu, NjNbT, NJQ, NN, NNC, NNNGB, NSmB, OCl, OClWHi.

Versteeg, Dingman. Flatlands Reformed Dutch Church baptisms, 1747-1802. (MS. and microfilm copy of MS.)   [802
NNHol.

———— Records of the Reformed Protestant Dutch Church of Gravesend.
(MS.)   [803
NNHol.

———— Records of the Reformed Dutch Church of Jamaica. Baptisms,
1702-1805.   (MS.)   [804
NNHol.

———— Records of the Reformed Dutch Church of Newtown. Baptisms,
1736-1845; members, 1739-1802; officers, 1736-1802. (MS.)   [805
NNHol.

———— Records of the Reformed Dutch Church of Success (Manhasset,
New York). Baptisms, 1742-1793; members, 1756-1776; various rec-
ords, 1732-1813.   (MS.)   [806
NNHol.

Vieth, Isaac. Williamsburgh: Book of reference, showing the location of
each lot, with farm numbers, etc. 1845.   [807
NBLiHi.

Voris, Maude E. Inscriptions from the Velsor cemetery at Syosset.
(Typed.)   [808
NBLiHi.

Waller, Henry Davey. History of the town of Flushing.   [809
Includes list of inhabitants, 1698 and muster roll of 1715.
CSmH, DLC, MB, N, NB, NBLiHi, NEh, NJQ, NN, NNNGB, NRvS, NSmB, OClWHi,
PHi.

Warriner, Rev. Edwin. Old Sands Street Methodist Episcopal church of
Brooklyn, New York (First Methodist Episcopal Church). Biographi-
cal records of early members and genealogical notes. 1885.   [810
DLC, MBNEH, NBLiHi, NJQ, NN, NNNGB.

———— First century of Methodism in Patchogue, 1791-1891. (Typed.)
Brief family sketches of early members.   [811
NJQ.

Waters, I. S. Extracts from the records of the Reformed church at Newtown, translated from the Dutch language. In *Putnam's Monthly Historical Magazine*, n.s., *2*, pp. 115-118.   [812
Ct, CtHi, CtY, DLC, ICN, In, MB, Mi, N, NBLiHi, Nh, NN, OCl, OClWHi, WHi.

Watkins, Walter Kendall. Some early New York settlers from New Eng-
land. In *New Eng. Hist. Geneal. Register, 55*, pp. 297-303, 377-381. [813
Az, C, CL, CoD, CSt, Ct, CtHi, CtHT, CtY, CU, DCU, DLC, DNDAR, GA, GHi, ICN,
ICU, In, InI, IU, KHi, KyLoF, M, MB, MBAt, MBC, MBNEH, MdBE, MdBP, Me,
MeB, MeBa, MeHi, MeP, MH, MHi, Mi, MiD-B, MiGr, MiMu, MiU, MiU-C, MNF,
MnHi, MoK, MoS, MPB, MWA, MWiW, N, NHLiHi, NbO, NBu, Nc, NEh, NhD, NHi,
NIC, NjP, NjPla, NJQ, NjR, NN, NNC, NNNGB, NNS, NNU-H, NR, OC, OCHP,
OCl, OClWHi, OHi, OMC, OrP, PEa, PEr, PHi, PPi, PPL, PWb, RP, T, TC, Tx,
USlGS, Vi, Wa, WaS, WHi, WM.

Weeks, Archibald C. Brookhaven town records (1662-1679). Copied, annotated and compiled by Archibald C. Weeks. 1924.   [814
DLC, DNDAR, MBNEH, N, NBB, NBLiHi, NEh, NJQ, NN, NNNGB, NRvS, ODW, USlGS.

Weeks, George Lewis. Some of Islip's Early History. (Islip, New York.) 1955.   [815
DLC, NBLiHi, NEh, NJQ, NN, NNNGB.

Weeks, James H. Papers, 1824-95. (MS.)   [816
Includes papers of William J. Weeks: Church records of Cold Spring; Christ Church, Oyster Bay; South Haven Church; St. Andrew's Church, Yaphank; the Long Island Railroad; roads and schools; receipts and payments to teachers and library funds.
NJQ.

Weeks, William J., and others. Records of the town of Brookhaven, New York, transcribed by William J. Weeks and others, and edited by Osborn Shaw. 1930-1932. Book A, 1657-1679 and 1790-1798; Book B, 1679-1756; Book C, 1687-1879.   [817
DLC, MBNEH, NBLiHi, NEh, NJQ, NN, NNNGB.

Weld, Ralph Foster. Brooklyn village, 1816-1834. 1938.   [818
DLC, MB, NBLiHi, NEh, NN, NNNGB.

Wells, Rev. Eurystheus Howell. Cemetery records, Old Steeple Church cemetery, Aquebogue, 1755-1868. 1868.   [819
NNNGB (photostat); NRvS (MS.).

————— Cemetery inscriptions of Upper Aquebogue, 1755-1866. (Typed notebook by the Rev. E. Howell Wells, copied by G. F. R. Albertson.)
NBLiHi, NN (MS.).   [820

Wendelken and Co. Atlas of the town of Babylon, Islip and south part of Brookhaven, in Suffolk County, New York, engraved and printed by L. E. Neuman and Co. 1888.   [821
DLC, NBLiHi, NHu, NJQ.

Werner, Charles J(olly). Genealogies of Long Island families, mainly from records compiled by Benjamin F. Thompson. 1919.   [822
DLC, DNDAR, MB, MBNEH, MWA, N, NBLiHi, NEh, NJQ, NN, NNNGB, NSmB, OClWHi, PHi, USlGS.

Wheat, Edwin Webb. Brookhaven relationships as deduced from *Records, Town of Brookhaven up to 1800.* 1933. (Typed.)   [823
NBLiHi.

————— Index to the vital records, 1648-1813, in the printed town records of Southampton. (Typed.)   [824
NBLiHi.

————— Suffolk County, New York. Index to wills to 31 December, 1850. (Typed.)   [825
NBLiHi.

Whitaker, Epher. History of Southold, its first century, 1640-1740. 1881, revised by Charles E. Craven in 1931. [826

DLC, DNDAR, MB, MWA, N, NBLiHi, NEh, NHu, NJQ, NN, NNNGB, NRvS, NSmB, OCl.

White, Alfred T. St. George's Episcopal churchyard, Hempstead, New York. (Inscriptions.) (Typed.) [827

NBLiHi.

White, Arthur. Records of the Presbyterian Church, Newtown (now Elmhurst), Queens County, Long Island, New York. In *New York Geneal. and Biog. Record, 55,* pp. 162, 281, 393; *56,* pp. 73, 173, 353. [828

Az, C, CaOTP, CL, CoD, CSf, Ct, CtHi, CtY, DLC, DNDAR, IaHi, IC, ICN, ICU, In, MB, MBAt, MBNEH, MdBP, MeHi, MH, MHi, Mi, MiD-B, MNF, MnHi, MnM, MoK, MoS, MWA, N, NB, NBLiHi, NBu, NBuG, Nc, NEh, Nh, NHC, NHi, NIC, NjNbS, NjPla, NJQ, NN, NNC, NNNGB, NR, OC, OCHP, OCl, OClWHi, OHi, PEa, PEr, PHi, PPi, PPL, USlGS, Wa, WaS, WM.

Also published separately as *Collections of the New York Geneal. and Biog. Society,* vol. 8. 1928.

DLC DNDAR, MB, MBNEH, MWA, NBLiHi, NBuG, NEh, NjP, NJQ, NN, NNNGB, USlGS.

Whittemore, Henry. Long Island historic homes, ancient and modern, including a history of their founders and builders. 1901. [829

NBLiHi, NEh, NN, NNNGB.

Wickham, Julia. Old Cutchogue cemetery inscriptions. (Typed.) [830

NBLiHi, NNNGB.

Wikoff, Helen Lyons. Conklin cemetery (inscriptions) . . . between Wyandanch and Melville. (Typed.) [831

NBLiHi.

Willard, James LeBaron. Long Island Genealogies. (MS.) [832

NBLiHi.

Wilson, John Ewell. Index to the wills of Queens County, New York, 1787-1906. (Typed.) [833

NJQ, NNNGB (microfilm).

———— Index of administrations of Queens County, New York, 1707-1908. (Typed.) [834

This index is to records in the Court House, Jamaica, New York.

NJQ.

Winans, George W(oodruff). Narrative history of its 280 years of service: The First Presbyterian Church of Jamaica, New York. 1662-1942. 1943. [835

MBNEH, NBLiHi, NJQ, NN.

Wolverton, Chester. Atlas of Queens County, Long Island, New York, compiled from official records, private plans and actual surveys. 1891.

NBLiHi, NJQ, NN. [836

Wood, Silas. Sketch of the town of Huntington, Long Island, from its first settlement to the end of the American revolution; edited with genealogical and historical notes by William S. Pelletreau. 1898.   [837
DLC, MWA, N, NBLiHi, NHu, NJQ, NN, NNC, NNNGB, NSmB.

Wood, Simeon. A history of Hauppauge, Long Island, New York, together with genealogies. Edited by Charles J(olly) Werner. 1920.   [838
DLC, DNDAR, MWA, N, NBLiHi, NEh, NHu, NJQ, NN, NNNGB, NRvS, NSmB, OClWHi, USlGS.

Woodworth, George H. Address book and deaths, 1877-1930. Brooklyn, New York. (MS.)   [839
NBLiHi.

Wyckoff, William F. Cemetery inscriptions from manuscripts in the possession of Mr. William F. Wyckoff of Jamaica, New York. Typed by Josephine C. Frost, 1912.   [840
(Being the first three volumes of *Long Island Cem. Inscriptions*.)
DLC, MBNEH, NBLiHi, NJQ, NNNGB.

————— Oyster Bay. Cemetery inscriptions; Fort Hill cemetery and Wortman cemetery. Typed by Josephine C. Frost.   [841
DLC.

Young, Selah, Jr. Records of the First Church of Southold. (MS.)   [842
NBLiHi.

Youngs, Florence Evelyn. Parish records of St. George's Episcopal Church, Flushing, 1782-1834. 1937. (Typed.)   [843
NBLiHi, NNNGB.

Also printed in *St. George's Sword and Shield,* December, 1905; baptisms, 1788-1834, marriages, 1782-1834, and burials, 1790-1834.
NBLiHi, NJQ, NN, NNNGB.

————— Long Island family genealogies, taken from family Bibles, church records, deeds and other similar material. Includes the baptismal records of the Reformed Dutch church of Wolver Hollow, Long Island. 1923?   [844
DLC.

————— Contents of Session Book No. 1, 1669-1687, Riverhead, Suffolk County, New York. (Typed.)   [845
NBLiHi, NNNGB.

PART II

PLACES

(With Reference to Bibliographical Sources listed in Part I)

BAY SHORE
Directories: 318

BAYSIDE
Cemetery inscriptions: 301

BAYVILLE
Cemetery inscriptions: 301
Vital records: 772

BEDFORD
Local history: 544

BELLEROSE
Vital records: 772

BELLE TERRE
Cemetery inscriptions: 691
Vital records: 772

BELLPORT
Cemetery inscriptions: 494, 691
Church records: 460
Vital records: 772

BETHPAGE
Cemetery inscriptions: 63, 64, 201, 493, 519, 547, 744, 754

BLISSVILLE
Directories: 753

BLUE POINT
Cemetery inscriptions: 691

BRENTWOOD
Cemetery inscriptions: 187
Genealogical compendiums: 191

BRIDGEHAMPTON
Cemetery inscriptions: 9, 331
Church records: 77, 359
Court records: 76
Local history: 358

BRIGHTWATERS
Directories: 318
Vital records: 772

BROOKHAVEN (town and village)
Atlases: 821
Cemetery inscriptions: 202, 203, 204, 205, 206, 207, 208, 209, 210, 211, 212, 213, 236, 331, 437, 480, 494, 654, 691, 791,793
Census: 281, 543, 637, 759, 760
Local history: 536
Military records: 693
Tax and assessment lists: 543
Town records: 79, 80, 414, 416, 814, 817
Vital records: 166, 236, 772
Wills and administrations: 81, 603
Miscellaneous: 692, 751, 823

BROOKLYN (town, village, city and borough)

Atlases: 83, 311, 383, 415, 600, 601, 659, 660, 661, 676, 821

Cemetery inscriptions: 84, 100, 110, 159, 194, 222, 301, 341, 517, 518, 664

Censuses: 543, 759, 760

Church records: 56, 85, 86, 87, 89, 93, 94, 95, 96, 97, 98, 101, 102, 103, 104, 109, 111, 112, 113, 114, 115, 116, 117, 118, 119, 120, 121, 249, 285, 396, 456, 468, 717, 727, 734, 737, 750, 773a, 810

Deeds: 92, 286

Directories: 72, 74, 88, 463

Lists of inhabitants: 105, 543

Local history: 17, 18, 67, 99, 131, 169, 170, 182, 248, 312, 313, 357, 579, 712, 818

Military records: 55, 702, 766, 767

Tax and assessment lists: 82, 391, 543

Town and court records (unpublished): At Kings County Clerk's office

Vital records: 90, 91, 107, 108, 310, 392, 393, 394, 395, 453, 677, 678, 772, 784, 839

Miscellaneous: 106, 474, 500, 589, 799

BROOKLYN MANOR

Directories: 631

BROOKVILLE

Vital records: 772

BUSHWICK (town and village)

Cemetery inscriptions: 48, 49, 125, 126, 129, 709

Censuses: 543, 759, 760

Church records: 89, 127, 128

Genealogical compendiums: 615

Lists of inhabitants: 543

Tax and assessment lists: 543

Town records: 785

Vital records: 397

Miscellaneous: 19

CANAAN LAKE

Cemetery inscriptions: 691

CANARSIE

Cemetery inscriptions: 214, 222

CANOE PLACE

Cemetery inscriptions: 494

CEDARHURST

Vital records: 772

CEDAR SWAMP

Miscellaneous: 140

CENTEREACH

Cemetery inscriptions: 494, 691

CENTERPORT

Cemetery inscriptions: 152

CENTRAL ISLIP

Local history: 192

CENTRAL PARK

Cemetery inscriptions: 493, 745

CENTRE ISLAND
Vital records: 772

CENTRE MORICHES
Cemetery inscriptions: 136, 494, 691

COLD SPRING
Cemetery inscriptions: 301
Church records: 816

COLD SPRING HARBOR
Cemetery inscriptions: 150, 160, 301
Local history: 161

COLLEGE POINT
Vital records: 772

COMMACK
Cemetery inscriptions: 152, 188, 494, 655

CORAM (MIDDLE TOWN)
Cemetery inscriptions: 236, 494 654, 691, 791, 792, 793

COW NECK
Vital Records: 772

CRAB MEADOW
Cemetery inscriptions: 148, 152

CUTCHOGUE
Cemetery inscriptions: 331, 398, 494, 830
Church records: 320, 428, 699
Vital records: 146, 320

DEER PARK
Local history: 193

DERING HARBOR
Vital records: 772

DIX (DICKS) HILLS
Cemetery inscriptions: 30, 152, 492, 494

DOUGLASTON
Cemetery inscriptions: 342

DUTCH KILLS (LONG ISLAND CITY)
Directories: 753

EAST HAMPTON (town and village)
Cemetery inscriptions: 152, 165, 171, 175, 240, 241, 331, 333, 338, 441, 442, 443, 444, 445, 494, 704
Censuses: 281, 759, 760
Church records: 362, 411, 599
Deeds: 604
Genealogical compendiums: 361, 625
Local history: 314, 315, 360, 361, 625
Military records: 412
Tax and assessment lists: 543
Town records: 362
Vital records: 166, 409, 772
Wills and administrations: 1, 2, 338

FISHER'S ISLAND
Local history: 254

FLANDERS
Cemetery inscriptions: 494

FLATBUSH (town and village)
Atlases: 185, 660, 676
Cemetery inscriptions: 215, 263, 265a, 287, 301
Censuses: 543, 759, 760
Church records: 266, 288, 682
Deeds: 264
Lists of inhabitants: 543
Local history: 701, 724, 725, 726, 801
Military records: 767
Tax and assessment lists: 265, 543
Town and court records (unpublished): At Kings County Clerk's office
Town records: 786
Vital records: 397, 772

FLATLANDS (NEW AMERSFOORT) (town and village)
Atlases: 185, 660
Cemetery inscriptions: 268, 301, 457
Censuses: 512, 543, 759, 760
Church records: 269, 302, 728, 735, 802
Lists of inhabitants: 543
Local history: 186, 800
Military records: 767
Tax and assessment lists: 543
Vital records: 397, 772
Miscellaneous: 43, 267, 269

FLORAL PARK
Directories: 662
Local history: 616
Vital records: 772

FLOWER HILL
Cemetery inscriptions: 301
Vital records: 772

FLUSHING (town and village)
Cemetery inscriptions: 301, 350, 366, 667, 668
Censuses: 759, 760
Church records: 275, 276, 277, 289, 290, 343, 344, 345, 346, 347, 348, 431, 554, 563, 843
Deeds: 272
Directories: 73, 271, 630, 756
Lists of inhabitants: 543, 809
Local history: 467, 483, 782, 809
Marriage licenses and intentions: 216
Military records: 278, 809
Tax and assessment lists: 543, 548
Town records: 279 (early town and court records destroyed)
Vital records: 273, 274, 289, 384, 772
Miscellaneous: 70, 71, 340, 773

FOREST HILLS
Directories: 498

FOREST PARK
Directories: 631

FORT SALONGA
Cemetery inscriptions: 152

FOSTER'S MEADOW (VALLEY STREAM)
Lists of inhabitants: 556

FREEPORT
Cemetery inscriptions: 217, 283, 301
Directories: 466, 609
Vital records: 772

FREETOWN
Cemetery inscriptions: 494

GARDEN CITY
Directories: 662
Vital records: 772

GARDINER'S ISLAND
Cemetery inscriptions: 152
Local history: 316

GLEN COVE
Cemetery inscriptions: 69, 301
Directories: 609
Vital records: 772

GLEN HEAD
Cemetery inscriptions: 301

GOWANUS (GOUANES)
Local history: 32
Miscellaneous: 167

GRAVESEND (town and village)
Atlases: 185, 660
Cemetery inscriptions: 51, 301, 458
Censuses: 543, 759, 760
Church records: 718, 803
Lists of inhabitants: 543
Local history: 716
Military records: 767
Tax and assessment lists: 319, 543
Town records: 29, 291 (unpublished town records at Kings County Clerk's office)
Vital records: 50, 729, 772

GREAT NECK
Cemetery inscriptions: 301, 638, 639
Directories: 611, 662
Vital records: 772

GREAT NECK ESTATES
Vital records: 772

GREAT NECK PLAZA
Vital records: 772

GREENLAWN
Cemetery inscriptions: 149, 152, 494

GREENPORT
Cemetery inscriptions: 400
Vital records: 772

GREENVALE
Cemetery inscriptions: 301

HALF HOLLOW HILLS
Cemetery Inscriptions: 494, 794

HAMPTON BAYS
Cemetery inscriptions: 494

HAUPPAUGE
Cemetery inscriptions: 494, 656
Genealogical compendiums: 838
Local history: 838

HEAD OF THE HARBOR
Vital records: 772

HEMPSTEAD (SOUTH HEMPSTEAD) (town and village)
Cemetery inscriptions: 218, 260, 292, 301, 351, 352, 827
Censuses: 552, 759, 760
Church records: 261, 262, 293, 294, 330, 370, 373, 505, 550, 551
Court records: 163
Directories: 466, 609, 662
Lists of inhabitants: 543
Local history: 507, 511, 549, 684
Tax and assessment lists: 543, 553
Town records: 374
Vital records: 163, 164, 577, 772
Miscellaneous: 368, 369

HEWLETT
Church records: 219, 372

HEWLETT BAY PARK
Vital records: 772

HEWLETT HARBOR
Vital records: 772

HEWLETT NECK
Vital records: 772

HICKSVILLE
Cemetery inscriptions: 301

HITHER PLAINS (MONTAUK)
Cemetery inscriptions: 494

HOLLIS
Directories: 497

HOLTSVILLE
Cemetery inscriptions: 654, 691

HOPEDALE
Cemetery inscriptions: 301

HUNTER'S POINT (LONG ISLAND CITY)
Directories: 753

HUNTINGTON (town and village)
Bibliography: 674
Cemetery inscriptions: 41, 152, 157, 158, 220, 295, 301, 334, 418, 433, 494, 503, 642, 794
Censuses: 759, 760
Church records: 407, 487, 505, 591, 641, 685
Court records: 408
Deeds: 640
Directories: 130
Genealogical compendiums: 686
Local history: 432, 608, 675, 837
Tax and assessment records: 543
Town records: 408, 674, 723
Vital records: 3, 427, 772
Miscellaneous: 40, 141, 607

HUNTINGTON BAY
Vital records: 772

HUNTINGTON SOUTH
Cemetery inscriptions: 494

ISLAND PARK
Vital records: 772

ISLIP (precinct, town and village)
Atlases: 821
Censuses: 281, 643, 759, 760
Lists of inhabitants: 419
Local history: 815
Town records (unpublished): At Town Hall, Islip
Vital records: 772

JAMAICA (town and village)
Cemetery inscriptions: 65, 222, 296, 301, 421
Censuses: 759, 760
Church records: 297, 298, 325, 462, 481, 554, 555, 556, 557, 558, 559, 612, 681, 804
Court records: 75
Directories: 15, 497, 756
Genealogical compendiums: 20, 21
Lists of inhabitants: 327
Local history: 325, 835
Tax and assessment lists: 420, 481, 543, 560
Town records: 299, 424
Village records: 426
Vital records: 75, 172, 772
Wills and administrations: 425
Miscellaneous: 422, 423

JAMESPORT (LOWER AQUEBOGUE)
Cemetery inscriptions: 331, 698

JERICHO

Cemetery inscriptions: 301, 350
Church records: 300, 349

JERUSALEM

Cemetery inscriptions: 493, 502
Local history: 280

KENSINGTON

Vital records: 772

KESKACHAUGE (FLATLANDS)

Local history: 800

KEW GARDENS

Directories: 498

KINGS COUNTY

Atlases: 415, 658
Cemetery inscriptions: 222, 452
Census records: 528, 762
Church records: 52, 523, 730
Deeds: 286, 488
Genealogical compendiums: 54, 250, 635
Local History: 170, 184, 579, 713
Military and civil lists: 543, 575
Tax and assessment lists: 451
Town records: 52
Vital records: 453, 772
Wills and administrations: 33, 53, 455, 489, 522, 748, 787
Miscellaneous: 78, 454, 521, 606, 721, 746, 771, 783

See also: Brooklyn, Bushwick, Flatbush, Flatlands, Gravesend, New Lots, New Utrecht.

KINGS PARK

Cemetery inscriptions: 152, 301

KINGS POINT

Vital records: 772

LAKE GROVE

Cemetery inscriptions: 205, 654, 691
Church records: 464, 661

LAKE RONKONKOMA

Cemetery inscriptions: 494, 654, 691

LAKE SUCCESS

Vital records: 772

LATTINGTOWN

Cemetery inscriptions: 301, 580
Vital records: 772

LAURELTON

Vital records: 772

LAWRENCE

Cemetery inscriptions: 301
Vital records: 772

LINDENHURST
Vital records: 772

LITTLE NECK
Cemetery inscriptions: 301
Directories: 662
Local history: 282

LLOYD'S HARBOR
Vital records: 772

LLOYD'S NECK
Cemetery inscriptions: 220

LOCUST VALLEY
Cemetery inscriptions: 301, 580, 758

LONG BEACH
Vital records: 772

LONG ISLAND
Atlases: 45
Bibliography: 561, 687, 771
Cemetery inscriptions: 4, 301, 331, 840
Censuses: 759, 760, 761, 763a, 768
Church records: 239, 523, 563
Court records: 257, 379, 380, 715
Deeds: 470, 541
Directories: 47, 74, 463, 469
Genealogical compendiums: 56, 57, 123, 124, 153, 162, 169, 223, 238, 250, 329, 371, 376, 413, 476, 485, 597, 598, 628, 690, 822, 832, 844
Lists of inhabitants: 379
Local history: 238, 245, 270, 357, 471, 562, 613, 657, 665, 666, 719, 749, 829, 832
Marriage licenses: 387, 435, 436, 527, 529, 542
Military records: 55, 258, 485, 764, 768, 769, 770
Vital records: 22, 23, 310, 401, 406, 449, 473, 475, 524, 525, 526, 626, 677, 678, 731
Wills and administrations: 227, 255, 477, 522, 593, 679
Miscellaneous: 256, 326, 380, 381, 448, 474, 540, 578, 757, 813, 816
See also: Kings county, Nassau county, Queens county and Suffolk county.

LONG ISLAND CITY
Directories: 472, 711, 753, 756
Local history: 439
Vital records: 772

LOWER AQUEBOGUE (see JAMESPORT)

LYNBROOK
Cemetery inscriptions: 224, 242
Church records: 644
Directories: 609
Vital records: 772

MALVERNE
Vital records: 772

MANHASSET (SUCCESS)
Cemetery inscriptions: 301, 350, 353
Church records: 564, 565, 566, 567, 806
Directories: 611, 662

MANORHAVEN
Vital records: 772

MANORVILLE
Cemetery inscriptions: 152, 494, 691

MASSAPEQUA
Cemetery inscriptions: 484, 493

MASSAPEQUA PARK
Vital records: 772

MASTIC NECK
Cemetery inscriptions: 494, 691

MATINECOCK
Cemetery inscriptions: 301, 350, 580
Vital records: 772

MATTITUCK
Cemetery inscriptions: 168, 301, 331
Church records: 168, 605
Directories: 486
Local history: 168

MEADOW BROOK
Cemetery inscriptions: 301

MECOX
Cemetery inscriptions: 152

MELVILLE
Cemetery inscriptions: 152, 220, 331, 494, 831
Church records: 495

MERRICK
Local history: 440

MIDDLE ISLAND
Cemetery inscriptions: 225, 494, 501, 691
Church records: 700

MIDDLEVILLE
Cemetery inscriptions: 152

MILLERS PLACE
Cemetery inscriptions: 206, 494, 691

MILL NECK
Cemetery inscriptions: 301, 580
Vital records: 772

MINEOLA
Directories: 662
Vital records: 772

MONTAUK
Cemetery inscriptions: 183, 494
Deeds: 506

MORICHES (patentship and village)
Cemetery inscriptions: 494
Censuses: 281
Military records: 693

MORRIS PARK
Directories: 631

MOUNT SINAI (OLD MANS)
Cemetery inscriptions: 208, 236, 331, 494, 654, 691
Vital records: 513

MUNSEY PARK
Vital records: 772

MUTTONTOWN (SPRING HILL)
Cemetery inscriptions: 301, 490
Vital records: 772

NASSAU COUNTY (Part of Queens Co. before 1899)
Cemetery inscriptions: 150, 493, 519
Censuses: 66, 528
Directories: 469
Local history: 28, 357
Vital records: 772
Wills and administrations: 522
See also: Hempstead (South Hempstead), North Hempstead, Oyster Bay.

NEW AMERSFOORT (AMESVOORT) (see FLATLANDS)
Miscellaneous: 167

NEW HYDE PARK
Vital records: 772

NEW LOTS (town and village) (originally in Flatbush town)
Atlases: 185
Cemetery inscriptions: 58, 195, 301
Censuses: 759
Church records: 520
Military records: 767
Vital records: 772

NEWTOWN (town and village)
Cemetery inscriptions: 301, 354, 355, 356, 367, 490
Censuses: 317, 759, 760
Church records: 179, 180, 530, 533, 556, 568, 805, 812, 828
Court records: 774
Genealogical compendiums: 24, 633
Local history: 417
Military records: 531
Tax and assessment lists: 535, 543, 569
Town records: 132, 416a, 534, 545, 775
Vital records: 772
Miscellaneous: 532, 546, 634

New Utrecht (town and village)
Atlases: 185, 660
Cemetery inscriptions: 60, 62, 222, 226, 301, 331, 402, 459
Censuses: 543, 759, 760
Church records: 302, 324, 738
Court records: 365
Genealogical compendiums: 59
Lists of inhabitants: 543
Local history: 32, 543
Military records: 767
Tax and assessment lists: 543
Vital records: 454, 729, 772
Miscellaneous: 61, 167, 732

New Village
Cemetery inscriptions: 494

Nissequogue
Cemetery inscriptions: 152
Vital records: 772

North Beach
Cemetery inscriptions: 34, 301, 668, 722
Directories: 753

North Haven
Cemetery inscriptions: 494, 778
Vital records: 772

North Hempstead (town: originally a part of Hempstead town)
Censuses: 759, 760
Church records: 538
Court records: 163
Tax and assessment lists: 537
Town records: 374
Vital records: 163, 164, 772

North Hills
Vital records: 772

North Mastic
Cemetery inscriptions: 691

Northport
Cemetery inscriptions: 42, 152, 494
Directory: 130
Vital records: 602, 772

North Sea
Cemetery inscriptions: 494

Northville
Cemetery inscriptions: 403
Vital records: 772

Northwest Harbor (East Hampton)
Cemetery inscriptions: 494

Oakdale
Cemetery inscriptions: 5, 494

OCEAN BEACH
Vital records: 772

OLD BROOKVILLE
Vital records: 772

OLD FIELD
Cemetery inscriptions: 494
Vital records: 772

OLD WESTBURY
Vital records: 772

ORIENT
Cemetery inscriptions: 11, 335, 450

ORIENT POINT
Cemetery inscriptions: 405, 494

OYSTER BAY (town and village)
Cemetery inscriptions: 150, 301, 303, 490, 514, 580, 583, 722, 841
Censuses: 759, 760
Church records: 68, 134, 154, 239, 304, 363, 364, 570, 722, 816
Genealogical compendiums: 722
Lists of inhabitants: 581, 582
Local history: 496
Tax and assessment lists: 543, 571
Town records: 156
Vital records: 772
Miscellaneous: 155, 340, 622

OYSTER BAY COVE
Cemetery inscriptions: 434
Vital records: 772

OZONE PARK
Directories: 498, 631

PATCHOGUE
Cemetery inscriptions: 152, 494, 654, 691
Church records: 811
Directories: 588
Vital records: 772

PEQUOTT
Vital records: 772

PLAINEDGE
Cemetery inscriptions: 493

PLAINVIEW
Cemetery inscriptions: 493, 519

PLANDOME
Directories: 611, 662
Vital records: 772

PLANDOME HEIGHTS
Vital records: 772

PLANDOME MANOR
Vital records: 772

PORT JEFFERSON
Cemetery inscriptions: 209, 494, 691
Town records: 79

PORT WASHINGTON and PORT WASHINGTON NORTH
Cemetery inscriptions: 14, 301, 493, 752
Vital records: 772

PROMISED LAND
Cemetery inscriptions: 614

QUEENS COUNTY and BOROUGH
Atlases: 836
Cemetery inscriptions: 222, 494a
Censuses: 196, 528
Church records: 523, 773a
Deeds: 328, 618, 621, 622, 623
Directories: 469, 609, 756
Genealogical compendiums: 144, 635
Lists of inhabitants: 378, 539, 573
Local history: 357, 515, 572, 617, 694, 710
Military records: 543, 574, 620, 765
Vital records: 406, 772
Wills and administrations: 44, 133, 137, 138, 221, 228, 425, 478, 490, 522, 621, 680, 833, 834
Miscellaneous: 617, 619, 622, 755
See also: Flushing, Hempstead (South Hempstead), Jamaica, Newtown, North Hempstead and Oyster Bay.

QUEENS VILLAGE (LLOYD'S NECK)
Directory: 497
Local history: 40, 578

QUOGUE
Cemetery inscriptions: 624
Vital records: 772
Miscellaneous: 610

RAVENSWOOD (LONG ISLAND CITY)
Directories: 753

RICHMOND HILL
Cemetery inscriptions: 301
Directories: 15, 498, 631, 756
Vital records: 772

RIDGE
Cemetery inscriptions: 494, 691

RIDGEWOOD
Local history: 280, 683

RIVERHEAD (town and village) (originally in Southold town)
Cemetery inscriptions: 229, 301, 306, 331, 645, 795
Censuses: 759, 760
Church records: 142, 143, 460, 461, 636
Court records: 590
Vital records: 772
Miscellaneous: 377

RIVERSIDE
    Cemetery inscriptions: 236

ROCKAWAY
    Cemetery inscriptions: 301
    Vital records: 772

ROCKAWAYS, THE
    Local history: 46

ROCKVILLE CENTRE
    Directories: 609
    Vital records: 772

ROCKY POINT
    Cemetery inscriptions: 210, 494, 691

ROSLYN
    Cemetery inscriptions: 150, 493
    Local history: 695
    Vital records: 772

ROSLYN ESTATES
    Vital records: 772

RUSSELL GARDENS
    Vital records: 772

SADDLE ROCK
    Vital records: 772

SAG HARBOR
    Cemetery inscriptions: 229, 331, 494, 669, 670, 671, 777, 778, 781
    Church records: 672, 779
    Local history: 696
    Vital records: 307, 772, 780
    Miscellaneous: 181, 584

SAINT JAMES
    Cemetery inscriptions: 494, 646

SALTAIRE
    Vital records: 772

SANDS POINT
    Cemetery inscriptions: 301, 585
    Vital records: 772

SAYVILLE
    Cemetery inscriptions: 494
    Local history: 246

SEA CLIFF
    Cemetery inscriptions: 493
    Vital records: 772

SEARINGTOWN
    Cemetery inscriptions: 135, 230, 493

SELDEN
    Cemetery inscriptions: 211, 494, 647, 654, 691, 792

SELLECK
Cemetery inscriptions: 580

SETAUKET
Cemetery inscriptions: 151, 231, 236, 301, 331, 438, 446, 447, 494, 654, 688, 691
Church records: 247, 320, 689
Miscellaneous: 751

SHELTER ISLAND (town and village)
Cemetery inscriptions: 331, 336, 338
Censuses: 281, 759, 760
Genealogical compendiums: 482
Local history: 190, 482, 578
Vital records: 323, 772

SHOREHAM
Cemetery inscriptions: 691
Vital records: 772

SMITH'S POINT
Cemetery inscriptions: 152, 691

SMITHTOWN (town and village)
Cemetery inscriptions: 152, 157, 158, 301, 308, 331, 494, 649
Census: 281, 759, 760
Church records: 31, 648
Lists of inhabitants: 632
Tax and assessment lists: 543
Town records: 122, 594, 697
Vital records: 772

SMITHTOWN BRANCH
Cemetery inscriptions: 494

SMITHTOWN LANDING (VILLAGE OF THE LANDING)
Cemetery inscriptions: 494

SOUTHAMPTON (town and village)
Cemetery inscriptions: 175, 232, 331, 587, 595, 704, 706
Censuses: 281, 705, 759, 760
Deeds: 6
Genealogical compendiums: 388
Lists of inhabitants: 543, 673
Local history: 10
Tax and assessment lists: 543
Town records: 707
Vital records: 166, 173, 174, 176, 177, 178, 389, 586, 772, 824

SOUTH BUSHWICK
Church records: 776

SOUTH FLORAL PARK
Vital records: 772

SOUTH GREENLAWN
Cemetery inscriptions: 152

SOUTH HAVEN
Cemetery inscriptions: 331, 480, 494, 691
Church records: 816

SOUTH HEMPSTEAD (town)

Cemetery inscriptions: 218
Censuses: 759, 760
Court records: 163
Town records: 374
Vital records: 163, 164
See also: Hempstead.

SOUTH HUNTINGTON

Cemetery inscriptions: 152, 418

SOUTH MANOR

Cemetery inscriptions: 494

SOUTHOLD (town and village)

Cemetery inscriptions: 301, 331, 337, 338, 404, 714
Censuses: 281, 759, 760
Church records: 410, 430, 788, 789, 842
Genealogical compendiums: 386, 509
Lists of inhabitants: 543
Local history: 321, 322, 429, 508, 826
Tax and assessment lists: 543
Town records: 139, 309
Vital records: 12, 147, 166, 323, 409, 504, 650, 651, 747, 772
Miscellaneous: 465, 708

SOUTH SETAUKET

Cemetery inscriptions: 691

SPRINGFIELD

Cemetery inscriptions: 233, 479
Miscellaneous: 234

SPRINGS, THE (EAST HAMPTON)

Cemetery inscriptions: 494

STEINWAY

Cemetery inscriptions: 35
Directories: 753

STEWART MANOR

Vital records: 772

STONY BROOK

Cemetery inscriptions: 213, 494, 654, 691, 720

STRONG NECK

Cemetery inscriptions: 235, 236

SUFFOLK COUNTY

Atlases: 821
Bibliography: 629
Cemetery inscriptions: 152, 236, 480, 494, 499, 794
Censuses: 528, 763
Church records: 743
Court records: 845
Deeds: 7, 236, 653, 741, 790
Directories: 47, 469
Genealogical compendiums: 145, 652, 747
Lists of inhabitants: 543
Local history: 28, 357, 516, 596, 739

Military records: 575
Vital records: 13, 36, 37, 38, 236, 475, 772
Wills and administrations: 8, 237, 243, 510, 522, 592, 740, 796, 797, 825
Miscellaneous: 25, 742

SWEZEYTOWN
Cemetery inscriptions: 152, 494, 691

SYOSSET
Cemetery inscriptions: 150, 301, 808

THOMASTON
Vital records: 772

UNIONVILLE
Church records: 733

UNION COURSE
Directories: 631

UPPER AQUEBOGUE
Cemetery inscriptions: 698, 820

UPPER BROOKVILLE
Vital records: 772

VALLEY STREAM
Vital records: 772

VILLAGE OF THE BRANCH (SMITHTOWN BRANCH)
Vital records: 772

VILLAGE OF THE LANDING (SMITHTOWN LANDING)
Vital records: 772

WADING RIVER
Cemetery inscriptions: 301, 494, 691
Local history: 491

WAINSCOTT
Cemetery inscriptions: 339

WANTAGH
Local history: 280

WESTBURY
Cemetery inscriptions: 301, 350
Church records: 375, 576
Vital records: 772

WESTHAMPTON
Cemetery inscriptions: 331, 494

WESTHAMPTON BEACH
Local history: 663
Vital records: 772

WEST HILLS
Cemetery inscriptions: 220, 494

WEST ISLIP
Cemetery inscriptions: 494

PART III

ALPHABETIC LIST OF LIBRARY SYMBOLS

AU	Univ. of Alabama, University, Alabama
Az	Arizona State Dept. of Library and Archives, Phoenix, Ariz.
C	California State Library, Sacramento, Calif.
CaNSWA	Acadia University, Wolfville, Nova Scotia
CaOTP	Toronto Public Library, Toronto, Ontario
CaOTU	Univ. of Toronto, Toronto, Ontario
CaT	See CaOTP
CL	Los Angeles Pub. Library, Los Angeles, Calif.
CoD	Denver Public Library, Denver, Colo.
CoU	Univ. of Colorado, Boulder, Colo.
CSf	San Francisco Pub. Library, San Francisco, Calif.
CSmH	Henry E. Huntington Library, San Marino, Calif.
CSt	Stanford College Libraries, Stanford, Calif.
Ct	Connecticut State Library, Hartford, Conn.
CtHi	Connecticut Historical Society, Hartford, Conn.
CtHT	Trinity College, Hartford, Conn.
CtU	Univ. of Connecticut, Storrs, Conn.
CtW	Wesleyan University, Middletown, Conn.
CtY	Yale University, New Haven, Conn.
CU	Univ. of California, Berkeley, Calif.
DCU	Catholic Univ., Washington, D. C.
DLC	Library of Congress, Washington, D. C.
DN	U. S. Department of the Navy, Washington, D. C.
DNA	U. S. National Archives, Washington, D. C.
DNDAR	Daughters of the American Revolution Library, Washington, D. C.
DNGS	National Genealogical Society, Washington, D. C.
DNLM	National Library of Medicine, Washington, D. C.
DNR	See DN
DNW	National War College Library, Fort McNair, Washington, D. C.
DSI-M	Smithsonian Institution, National Museum, Washington, D. C.
GA	Atlanta Pub. Library, Atlanta, Georgia
GHi	Georgia Historical Society, Savannah, Georgia
I	Illinois State Library, Springfield, Ill.
IaHi	State Historical Society of Iowa, Iowa City, Iowa
IaU	State Univ. of Iowa, Iowa City, Iowa
IC	Chicago Public Library, Chicago, Ill.
ICHi	Chicago Historical Society, Chicago, Ill.
ICJ	John Crerar Library, Chicago, Ill.
ICN	Newberry Library, Chicago, Ill.
ICU	Univ. of Chicago, Chicago, Ill.
IEN	Northwestern Univ., Evanston, Ill.
IHi	Illinois State Historical Society, Springfield, Ill.

In	Indiana State Library, Indianapolis, Indiana
InI	Indianapolis Public Library, Indianapolis, Indiana
InThE	Emeline Fairbanks Memorial Library, Terre Haute, Indiana
InU	Indiana Univ., Bloomington, Indiana
IU	University of Illinois, Urbana, Illinois
KHi	Kansas State Historical Society, Topeka, Kansas
KyLoF	Filson Club, Louisville, Kentucky
M	Massachusetts State Library, Boston, Mass.
MA	Amherst College, Amherst, Mass.
MB	Boston Public Library, Boston, Mass.
MBAt	Boston Athenaeum, Boston, Mass.
MBC	Congregational Library, Boston, Mass.
MBNEH	New England Historic Genealogical Society, Boston, Mass.
MdBE	Enoch Pratt Library, Baltimore, Md.
MdBJ	Johns Hopkins University, Baltimore, Md.
MdBP	Peabody Institute, Baltimore, Md.
Me	Maine State Library, Augusta, Maine
MeB	Bowdoin College, Brunswick, Maine
MeBa	Bangor Public Library, Bangor, Maine
MeHi	Maine Historical Society, Portland, Maine
MeP	Portland Public Library, Portland, Maine
MeU	Univ. of Maine, Orono, Maine
MH	Harvard Univ., Cambridge, Mass.
MHi	Massachusetts Historical Society, Boston, Mass.
MH-L	Law School Library, Harvard Univ., Cambridge, Mass.
Mi	Michigan State Library, Lansing, Mich.
MiD	Detroit Public Library, Detroit, Michigan
MiD-B	Burton Historical Coll., Detroit Public Lib., Detroit, Mich.
MiGr	Grand Rapids Public Library, Grand Rapids, Mich.
MiHM	Michigan College of Mining and Technology, Houghton, Mich.
MiMu	Hackley Public Library, Muskegon, Mich.
MiU	Univ. of Michigan, Ann Arbor, Mich.
MiU-C	W. L. Clements Library, Univ. of Michigan, Ann Arbor, Mich.
MNF	Forbes Public Library, Northampton, Mass.
MnHi	Minnesota Historical Society, St. Paul, Minn.
MnM	Minneapolis Public Library, Minneapolis, Minn.
MNS	Smith College, Northampton, Mass.
MnU	Univ. of Minnesota, Minneapolis, Minn.
MoK	Kansas City Public Library, Kansas City, Mo.
MoS	St. Louis Pub. Library, St. Louis, Mo.
MoStj	St. Joseph Public Library, St. Joseph, Mo.
MPB	Berkshire Athenaeum, Pittsfield, Mass.
MS	City Library Association, Springfield, Mass.
MWA	American Antiquarian Society, Worcester, Mass.
MWiW	Williams College, Williamstown, Mass.
MWiW-C	Chapin Library, Williams College, Williamstown, Mass.
N	New York State Library, Albany, New York
NAu	Seymour Public Library, Auburn, New York
NB	Brooklyn Public Library, Brooklyn, New York

NBB	Brooklyn Museum Libraries, Brooklyn, New York
NBC	Brooklyn College, Brooklyn, New York
NBG	Brooklyn Botanic Garden, Brooklyn, New York
NBLiHi	Long Island Historical Society, Brooklyn, New York
NbO	Omaha Public Library, Omaha, Nebraska
NBP	Pratt Institute, Brooklyn, New York
NBu	Buffalo and Erie County Public Library, Buffalo, New York
NBuG	Grosvenor Reference Div., Buffalo and Erie Pub. Libr. Buffalo, N. Y.
Nc	North Carolina State Library, Raleigh, North Carolina
NcD	Duke University, Durham, North Carolina
NCH	Hamilton College, Clinton, New York
NcRS	North Car. State Coll. Agric. and Engin., Raleigh, N. C.
NcU	Univ. of North Carolina, Chapel Hill, North Carolina
NdU	Univ. of North Dakota, Grand Forks, North Dakota
NEh	East Hampton Free Library, East Hampton, New York
NGlc	Glen Cove Public Library, Glen Cove, N. Y.
Nh	New Hampshire State Library, Concord, New Hampshire
NHC	Colgate Univ., Hamilton, N. Y.
NhD	Dartmouth College, Hanover, New Hampshire
NHi	New York Historical Society, New York City, N. Y.
NHu	Huntington Public Library, Huntington, N. Y.
NHuHi	Huntington Historical Society, Huntington, N. Y.
NIC	Cornell University, Ithaca, New York
NIC-A	State Coll. of Agric., Cornell Univ., Ithaca, N. Y.
Nj	New Jersey State Library, Trenton, New Jersey
NjHi	New Jersey Historical Society, Newark, New Jersey
NjN	Newark Public Library, Newark, New Jersey
NjNbR	See NjR
NjNbS	Gardner A. Sage Library, New Brunswick, New Jersey
NjNbT	See NjNbS
NjO	Free Public Library of the City of Orange, N. J.
NjP	Princeton Univ., Princeton, New Jersey
NjPla	Plainfield Public Library, Plainfield, New Jersey
NJQ	Queens Borough Public Library, Jamaica, New York
NjR	Rutgers, the State Univ., New Brunswick, New Jersey
NN	New York Public Library, New York City, N. Y.
NNA	American Geographical Society, New York City, N. Y.
NNC	Columbia University, New York City, N. Y.
NNG	General Theological Seminary (Prot. Epis.), New York City, N. Y.
NNHi	See NHi
NNHol	Holland Society of New York, New York City, N. Y.
NNM	American Museum of Natural History, New York City, N. Y.
NNNGB	New York Genealogical and Biographical Society, New York City, N. Y.
NNQ	See NJQ
NNS	New York Society Library, New York City, N. Y.
NNU	New York Univ. Libraries, New York City, N. Y.

NNU-H	University Heights Library, New York Univ., New York City, N. Y.
NNUT	Union Theological Seminary, New York City, N. Y.
NPV	Vassar College, Poughkeepsie, New York
NR	Rochester Public Library, Rochester, New York
NRU	Univ. of Rochester, Rochester, New York
NRiHi	See NRvS
NRvS	Suffolk County Historical Society, Riverhead, New York
NSmB	Smithtown Public Library, Smithtown Branch, N. Y.
NStC	St. Bonaventure Univ., St. Bonaventure, New York
NSyU	Syracuse Univ., Syracuse, New York
NWM	U. S. Military Academy, West Point, New York
OC	Public Library of Cincinnati and Hamilton Co., Cincinnati, Ohio
OCHP	Historical and Philosophical Soc. of Ohio, Cincinnati, Ohio
OCl	Cleveland Public Library, Cleveland, Ohio
OClW	Western Reserve Univ., Cleveland, Ohio
OClWHi	Western Reserve Historical Society, Cleveland, Ohio
OCU	Univ. of Cincinnati, Cincinnati, Ohio
OCX	Xavier Univ., Cincinnati, Ohio
ODW	Ohio Wesleyan Univ., Delaware, Ohio
OFH	Hayes Memorial Library, Fremont, Ohio
OHi	Ohio State Historical Society, Columbus, Ohio
OMC	Marietta College, Marietta, Ohio
OO	Oberlin College, Oberlin, Ohio
OOxM	Miami Univ., Oxford, Ohio
OrP	Library Association of Portland, Portland, Ore.
OU	Ohio State Univ., Columbus, Ohio
OY	Public Library of Youngstown, Ohio
PBL	Lehigh Univ., Bethlehem, Penna.
PBMC	Moravian College and Theological Seminary, Bethlehem, Penna.
PCA	American Baptist Historical Society, Chester, Penna.
PEa	Easton Public Library, Easton, Penna.
PEr	Erie Public Library, Erie, Penna.
PHC	Haverford College, Haverford, Penna.
PHi	Historical Society of Pennsylvania, Philadelphia, Penna.
PMA	Allegheny College, Meadville, Penna.
PP	Free Library of Philadelphia, Philadelphia, Penna.
PPA	Athenaeum of Philadelphia, Philadelphia, Penna.
PPAmP	American Philosophical Society, Philadelphia, Penna.
PPFr	Friends Free Library of Germantown, Philadelphia, Penna.
PPG	German Society of Pennsylvania, Philadelphia, Penna.
PPi	Carnegie Library of Pittsburgh, Penna.
PPL	Library Company of Philadelphia, Philadelphia, Penna.
PPL-R	Ridgeway Branch, Library Co. of Philadelphia, Philadelphia, Penna.
PPLT	Lutheran Theological Seminary, Philadelphia, Penna.
PPPrHi	Presbyterian Historical Society, Philadelphia, Penna.
PPT	Temple Univ., Philadelphia, Penna.

PSC-Hi	Friends Hist. Library, Swarthmore College, Swarthmore, Penna.
PSt	Pennsylvania State Univ., University Park, Penna.
PU	Univ. of Pennsylvania, Philadelphia, Penna.
PU-L	Biddle Law Library, Univ. of Pennsylvania, Philadelphia, Penna.
PV	Villanova College, Villanova, Penna.
PWb	Osterhout Free Library, Wilkes-Barre, Penna.
PWcT	Pennsylvania State Teachers College, West Chester, Penna.
RHi	Rhode Island Historical Society, Providence, R. I.
RP	Providence Free Library, Providence, R. I.
RPJCB	John Carter Brown Library, Providence, R. I.
RWoU	L'Union Saint-Jean-Baptiste d'Amerique, Woonsocket, R. I.
ScC	Charleston Library Society, Charleston, South Carolina
T	Tennessee State Library, Nashville, Tennessee
TC	Chattanooga Public Library, Chattanooga, Tennessee
TU	Univ. of Tennessee, Knoxville, Tennessee
Tx	Texas State Library and Hist. Commission, Austin, Texas
TxU	Univ. of Texas, Austin, Texas
USlGS	Genealogical Society Library, Salt Lake City, Utah
Vi	Virginia State Library, Richmond, Virginia
ViU	Univ. of Virginia, Charlottesville, Virginia
ViW	College of William and Mary, Williamsburg, Virginia
Vt	Vermont State Library, Montpelier, Vermont
Wa	Washington State Library, Olympia, Washington
WaS	Seattle Public Library, Seattle, Washington
WaSp	Spokane Public Library, Spokane, Washington
WaU	Univ. of Washington, Seattle, Washington
WHi	State Historical Society of Wisconsin, Madison, Wisconsin
WM	Milwaukee Public Library, Milwaukee, Wis.

PART IV

ALPHABETIC LIST OF LIBRARIES

Acadia University, Wolfville, Nova Scotia	CaNSWA
Allegheny College, Meadville, Penna.	PMA
American Antiquarian Society, Worcester, Mass.	MWA
American Baptist Historical Society, Chester, Penna.	PCA
American Geographical Society, New York City, N. Y.	NNA
American Museum of Natural History, New York City, N. Y.	NNM
American Philosophical Society, Philadelphia, Penna.	PPAmP
Amherst College, Amherst, Mass.	MA
Arizona State Dept. of Library and Archives, Phoenix, Arizona	Az
Athenaeum of Philadelphia, Philadelphia, Penna.	PPA
Atlanta Public Library, Atlanta, Georgia	GA
Bangor Public Library, Bangor, Maine	MeBa
Berkshire Athenaeum, Pittsfield, Mass.	MPB
Boston Athenaeum, Boston, Mass.	MBAt
Boston Public Library, Boston, Mass.	MB
Bowdoin College, Brunswick, Maine	MeB
Brooklyn Botanic Garden, Brooklyn, New York	NBG
Brooklyn College, Brooklyn, New York	NBC
Brooklyn Museum Libraries, Brooklyn, New York	NBB
Brooklyn Public Library, Brooklyn, New York	NB
Buffalo and Erie County Public Library, Buffalo, New York	NBu
California State Library, Sacramento, California	C
Carnegie Library of Pittsburgh, Penna.	PPi
Catholic Univ. of America, Washington, D. C.	DCU
Charleston Library Society, Charleston, South Carolina	ScC
Chattanooga Public Library, Chattanooga, Tennessee	TC
Chicago Historical Society, Chicago, Ill.	ICHi
Chicago Public Library, Chicago, Illinois	IC
City Library Association, Springfield, Mass.	MS
Cleveland Public Library, Cleveland, Ohio	OCl
Colgate Univ., Hamilton, New York	NHC
College of William and Mary, Williamsburg, Virginia	ViW
Columbia University, New York City, New York	NNC
Congregational Library, Boston, Mass.	MBC
Connecticut Historical Society, Hartford, Conn.	CtHi
Connecticut State Library, Hartford, Conn.	Ct
Cornell University, Ithaca, New York	NIC
Cornell Univ., State Coll. Agric and Econ., Ithaca, N. Y.	NIC-A
Dartmouth College, Hanover, New Hampshire	NhD
Daughters of the American Revolution Library, Washington, D. C.	DNDAR
Denver Public Library, Denver, Colo.	CoD
Detroit Public Library, Detroit, Michigan	MiD

Detroit Pub. Library, Burton Historical Coll., Detroit, Mich.	MiD-B
Duke Univ., Durham, North Carolina	NcD
East Hampton Free Library, East Hampton, New York	NEh
Easton Public Library, Easton, Penna.	PEa
Emeline Fairbanks Mem. Library, Terre Haute, Indiana	InThE
Enoch Pratt Library, Baltimore, Md.	MdBE
Erie Public Library, Erie, Penna.	PEr
Filson Club, Louisville, Kentucky	KyLoF
Forbes Public Library, Northampton, Mass.	MNF
Free Library of Philadelphia, Philadelphia, Penna.	PP
Free Public Library of the City of Orange, N. J.	NjO
Friends Free Library of Germantown, Philadelphia, Penna.	PPFr
Gardner A. Sage Library, New Brunswick, New Jersey	NjNbS
Genealogical Society Library, Salt Lake City, Utah	USlGS
General Theological Seminary (Protestant Epis.),	
New York City, New York	NNG
Georgia Historical Society, Savannah, Georgia	GHi
German Society of Pennsylvania, Philadelphia, Penna.	PPG
Glen Cove Public Library, Glen Cove, New York	NGlc
Grand Rapids Public Library, Grand Rapids, Mich.	MiGr
Grosvenor Reference Div., Buffalo and Erie County Public	
Library, Buffalo, New York	NBuG
Hackley Public Library, Muskegon, Mich.	MiMu
Hamilton College, Clinton, New York	NCH
Harvard University, Cambridge, Mass.	MH
Harvard University, Law School Library, Cambridge, Mass.	MH-L
Haverford College, Haverford, Penna.	PHC
Hayes Memorial Library, Fremont, Ohio	OFH
Henry E. Huntington Library, San Marino, Calif.	CSmH
Historical and Philosophical Soc. of Ohio, Cincinnati, Ohio	OCHP
Historical Society of Pennsylvania, Philadelphia, Penna.	PHi
Holland Society of New York, New York City, New York	NNHol
Huntington Historical Society, Huntington, New York	NHuHi
Huntington Public Library, Huntington, New York	NHu
Illinois State Historical Society, Springfield, Illinois	IHi
Illinois State Library, Springfield, Illinois	I
Indiana State Library, Indianapolis, Indiana	In
Indiana University, Bloomington, Indiana	InU
Indianapolis Public Library, Indianapolis, Indiana	InI
John Carter Brown Library, Providence, Rhode Island	RPJCB
John Crerar Library, Chicago, Ill.	ICJ
Johns Hopkins Univ. Library, Baltimore, Md.	MdBJ
Kansas City Public Library, Kansas City, Missouri	MoK
Kansas State Historical Society, Topeka, Kansas	KHi
Lehigh Univ., Bethlehem, Penna.	PBL
Library Association of Portland, Portland, Ore.	OrP
Library Co. of Philadelphia, Philadelphia, Penna.	PPL
Library Co. of Phila., Ridgeway Branch, Philadelphia, Penna.	PPL-R

Long Island Historical Society, Brooklyn, New York — NBLiHi
Los Angeles Public Library, Los Angeles, Calif. — CL
L'Union Saint-Jean-Baptiste d'Amerique, Woonsocket, R. I. — RWoU
Lutheran Theological Seminary, Krauth Mem. Lib.,
   Philadelphia, Pa. — PPLT

Maine Historical Society, Portland, Maine — MeHi
Maine State Library, Augusta, Maine — Me
Marietta College, Marietta, Ohio — OMC
Massachusetts Historical Society, Boston, Mass. — MHi
Massachusetts State Library, Boston, Mass. — M
Miami Univ., Oxford, Ohio — OOxM
Michigan College of Mining and Technology,
   Houghton, Mich. — MiHM
Michigan State Library, Lansing, Michigan — Mi
Milwaukee Public Library, Milwaukee, Wisconsin — WM
Minneapolis Public Library, Minneapolis, Minn. — MnM
Minnesota Historical Society, St. Paul, Minn. — MnHi
Moravian College and Theol. Seminary, Bethlehem, Penna. — PBMC

National Genealogical Society Library, Washington, D. C. — DNGS
National Library of Medicine, Washington, D. C. — DNLM
Newark Public Library, Newark, N. J. — NjN
Newberry Library, Chicago, Illinois — ICN
New England Historic Genealogical Society, Boston, Mass. — MBNEH
New Hampshire State Library, Concord, New Hampshire — Nh
New Jersey Historical Society, Newark, New Jersey — NjHi
New Jersey State Library, Arch. and Hist., Trenton,
   New Jersey — Nj
New York Genealogical and Biographical Soc., New
   York City, New York — NNNGB
New York Historical Society, New York City, New York — NHi
New York Public Library, New York City, N. Y. — NN
New York Society Library, New York City, New York — NNS
New York State Library, Albany, New York — N
New York University Libraries, New York City, New York — NNU
New York Univ. Libraries, Univ. Heights Library,
   New York City, N. Y. — NNU-H
North Carolina State Coll. of Agric. and Engin., Raleigh, N. C. — NcRS
North Carolina State Library, Raleigh, N. C. — Nc
Northwestern University, Evanston, Illinois — IEN

Oberlin College, Oberlin, Ohio — OO
Ohio State Historical Society, Columbus, Ohio — OHi
Ohio State University, Columbus, Ohio — OU
Ohio Wesleyan Univ., Delaware, Ohio — ODW
Omaha Public Library, Omaha, Nebraska — NbO
Orange Free Public Library, Orange, New Jersey — NjO
Osterhout Free Library, Wilkes-Barre, Penna. — PWb

Peabody Institute, Baltimore, Md.	MdBP
Pennsylvania State Teachers College, West Chester, Penna.	PWcT
Pennsylvania State University, University Park, Penna.	PSt
Plainfield Public Library, Plainfield, New Jersey	NjPla
Portland Public Library, Portland, Maine	MeP
Pratt Institute, Brooklyn, New York	NBP
Presbyterian Historical Society, Philadelphia, Penna.	PPPrHi
Princeton Univ., Princeton, New Jersey	NjP
Providence Free Library, Providence, R. I.	RP
Public Library of Cincinnati and Hamilton Co., Cincinnati, Ohio	OC
Public Library of Youngstown, Ohio	OY
Queens Borough Public Library, Jamaica, New York	NJQ
Rhode Island Historical Society, Providence, R. I.	RHi
Rochester Public Library, Rochester, N. Y.	NR
Rutgers, the State Univ., New Brunswick, New Jersey	NjR
St. Bonaventure Univ., St. Bonaventure, New York	NStC
St. Joseph Public Library, St. Joseph, Missouri	MoStj
St. Louis Public Library, St. Louis, Missouri	MoS
San Francisco Public Library, San Francisco, Calif.	CSf
Seattle Public Library, Seattle, Washington	WaS
Seymour Public Library, Auburn, New York	NAu
Smith College, Northampton, Mass.	MNS
Smithsonian Institution Library, Nat. Museum Lib., Washington, D. C.	DSI-M
Smithtown Public Library, Smithtown Branch, New York	NSmB
Spokane Public Library, Spokane, Washington	WaSp
Stanford College Libraries, Stanford, Calif.	CSt
State Historical Soc. of Iowa, Iowa City, Iowa	IaHi
State Historical Society of Wisconsin, Madison, Wisconsin	WHi
State University of Iowa, Iowa City, Iowa	IaU
Suffolk County Historical Society, Riverhead, New York	NRvS
Swarthmore Col., Friends Historical Library, Swarthmore, Penna.	PSC-Hi
Syracuse University, Syracuse, New York	NSyU
Temple University, Philadelphia, Penna.	PPT
Tennessee State Library, Nashville, Tennessee	T
Texas State Library and Historical Com., Austin, Texas	Tx
Toronto Public Library, Toronto, Ontario	CaOTP
Trinity College, Hartford, Conn.	CtHT
Union Theological Seminary, New York City, New York	NNUT
United States Dept. of the Navy Library, Washington, D. C.	DN
″　　″　　Library of Congress, Washington, D. C.	DLC
″　　″　　Military Academy, West Point, New York	NWM
″　　″　　National Archives Library, Washington, D. C.	DNA
″　　″　　National War College Library, Fort McNair Wash'n, D. C.	DNW

University of Alabama, University, Alabama   AU
    ”   ” California, Berkeley, Calif.   CU
    ”   ” Chicago, Chicago, Ill.   ICU
    ”   ” Cincinnati, Cincinnati, Ohio   OCU
    ”   ” Colorado, Boulder, Colo.   CoU
    ”   ” Connecticut, Storrs, Conn.   CtU
    ”   ” Illinois, Urbana, Ill.   IU
    ”   ” Maine, Orono, Maine   MeU
    ”   ” Michigan, Ann Arbor, Mich.   MiU
    ”   ” Michigan, W. L. Clements Library, Ann Arbor,
                 Mich.   MiU-C
    ”   ” Minnesota, Minneapolis, Minn.   MnU
    ”   ” North Carolina, Chapel Hill, North Carolina   NcU
    ”   ” North Dakota, Grand Forks, North Dakota   NdU
    ”   ” Pennsylvania, Philadelphia, Penna.   PU
    ”   ” Pennsylvania, Biddle Law Library,
                 Philadelphia, Pa.   PU-L
    ”   ” Rochester, Rochester, New York   NRU
    ”   ” Tennessee, Knoxville, Tennessee   TU
    ”   ” Texas, Austin, Texas   TxU
    ”   ” Toronto, Toronto, Ontario   CaOTU
    ”   ” Virginia, Charlottesville, Virginia   ViU
    ”   ” Washington, Seattle, Washington   WaU

Vassar College, Poughkeepsie, New York   NPV
Vermont State Library, Montpelier, Vermont   Vt
Villanova College, Villanova, Penna.   PV
Virginia State Library, Richmond, Virginia   Vi

Washington State Library, Olympia, Washington   Wa
Wesleyan University, Middletown, Conn.   CtW
Western Reserve Historical Society, Cleveland, Ohio   OClWHi
Western Reserve University, Cleveland, Ohio   OClW
Williams College, Williamstown, Mass.   MWiW
    ”   ”   Chapin Library, Williamstown, Mass.   MWiW-C

Xavier Univ., Cincinnati, Ohio   OCX

Yale University, New Haven, Conn.   CtY